Democratic
Curriculum Leadership

Democratic Curriculum Leadership

Critical Awareness to Pragmatic Artistry

James G. Henderson, Daniel J. Castner,
and Jennifer L. Schneider

ROWMAN & LITTLEFIELD
Lanham • Boulder • New York • London

Published by Rowman & Littlefield
A wholly owned subsidiary of The Rowman & Littlefield Publishing Group, Inc.
4501 Forbes Boulevard, Suite 200, Lanham, Maryland 20706
www.rowman.com

Unit A, Whitacre Mews, 26-34 Stannary Street, London SE11 4AB

British Library Cataloguing in Publication Information Available

Library of Congress Cataloging-in-Publication Data Available

ISBN 978-1-4758-3786-5 (cloth : alk. paper)
ISBN 978-1-4758-3787-2 (pbk. : alk. paper)
ISBN 978-1-4758-3788-9 (electronic)

♾™ The paper used in this publication meets the minimum requirements of American
National Standard for Information Sciences—Permanence of Paper for Printed Library
Materials, ANSI/NISO Z39.48-1992.

Printed in the United States of America

We dedicate this book to the democratically-inspired educators who persevere each day with a deep sense of professional integrity. They rarely receive the heartfelt thanks they deserve. Working against the grain of a historical moment that delimits, depresses, and dehumanizes, their pursuit of professional excellence is impressive. Their commitment to practicing a holistic and democratic educational artistry has inspired this book. We hope that one day such high-minded educators will be the norm, not the exception. Our text has been written as an affirmation and celebration of this visionary future.

Contents

Preface

Welcome fellow educators and other interested readers to our book, which is dedicated to advancing education as a lead profession for societies with democratic aspirations. Our text provides theoretical and practical guidance on how to study and practice a curriculum problem-solving artistry that is focused on teaching for subject matter understandings that are deepened by democratic self and social understandings. We begin with a discussion of seven guiding principles of quality education, which will provide a foundational framework for the presentation of our theoretical platform.

The curriculum problem solving we are introducing and encouraging has four interrelated phases, and our advice on the study and practice of each phase has been organized into separate chapters using a montage format incorporating inquiry prompts, supportive quotations, critical commentaries, practical tips, narrative illustrations, and study recommendations. Because the four phases are folded into one another in highly interactive ways, we succinctly refer to our problem-solving approach as a *fourfold process*. Our text concludes with an epilogue honoring the journey of understanding and the pursuit of professional virtues that are central to the problem-solving discipline and artistry we are advocating. An ethical oath that was created by an Ohio teacher leader serves as a concrete expression of the disciplinary commitment that our book's interpretation of pedagogical excellence invites and requires.

The discussion of the seven principles in the introductory chapter and the presentation of our theoretical platform in chapter 1 are designed to offer much food for thought on the interrelationship between curriculum, teaching, and leadership in the enactment of democratic education. Assuming that your vocational calling is to be a democratic educator or that you are open to exploring such a professional identity, we hope you will find some degree of resonance with the ideas and guidance we are presenting. As you read this book, you may find yourself pondering some complex professional development issues; and you may possibly experience some ambivalence about what we're advocating. You may feel that the concepts promoted in this book are appealing as theoretical ideas, but for a number of reasons you wonder if they are realistic given our current educational policies and teacher management practices. How might educators actually work with the concepts we will be putting forth? What does our professional advice look like in action—on the ground in schools and in the daily lives of educators? Such questions, uncertainties, and hesitations are certainly warranted in a book that is based on a critical, visionary perspective on an educational problem solving that stands in contrast to standardized, bureaucratic decision-making. We will have much more to say on this topic in the introductory chapter and chapter 1.

We recognize that there are no easy answers on *how* to cultivate the problem-solving artistry we are advocating. Because the fourfold process is challenging and complex, the practical guidance we will be offering is not organized into a step-by-step format. Instead, we have organized our advice into four personally inviting montages. Moreover, what is found in our montage chapters is not designed to be followed in some lock-and-key manner. Studying our montages is not like reading directions on a roadmap, nor is it like doing a paint-by-number exercise. You are not being presented with a set of technical steps or a precise protocol that you should habitually follow. We are presenting a problem-solving process that, hopefully, will inspire you to be a critical and creative problem solver, practicing a holistic education that is grounded in the power of human understanding.

The fact that our fourfold process is not a simple, linear method shouldn't be surprising since uniformity, obedience, control, enforcement, formulas, and hierarchies fall outside the purview of democratic ethics. Critically pondering the contrasts between standardized ways of operating and the theory and practice of our fourfold process will be an important part of studying this book. The folding we are advancing can be compared to embarking on a twisting and turning journey through an inviting and somewhat mysterious mazeway. The goal is not to efficiently get through the maze but to embrace experiences that foster awakening, awareness, and critical insight.

To imagine this journey, direct your attention to "The Fourfold Process" figure. The figure illustrates a folding process that centers on you and your journey of holistic understanding, which is embedded in the interplay of particular interpretations of professional awakening, creative teaching, generative lead-learning, and participatory evaluating.

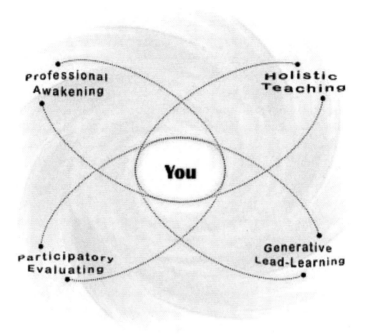

The Fourfold Process

The professional awakening, creative teaching, generative lead-learning, and participatory evaluating that we have in mind is grounded in a critical thinking that may challenge your current educational thoughts, perceptions, and actions. The fourfold process invites a disciplined, open-minded inquiry that is centered in continuous learning. You may need to disrupt the need to achieve final results and to control a future that is unpredictable; after all, you are on an exploratory journey of understanding.

In the problem solving we are advancing, "not always knowing" is not only okay; it's liberating. Our fourfold process encourages an awareness of the interplay of part and whole. Democratic education is a holistic undertaking, not a technical exercise. Technical prowess is important in any form of artistry, including the problem solving we are advancing. However, we are encouraging you to think ecologically about the fourfold process—to consider the ways that the pieces in this book are parts of a larger whole, and to recognize that the whole is ever present in the pieces. Folding is about humbly embracing personal journeys of understanding in which each one of us is an incomplete work-in-progress, living in a world of constantly moving parts. There are no all-knowing, authoritative masters of the problem-solving artistry we are encouraging. Those of us who are committed to the study, practice, and support of the fourfold process are engaged in a never-ending journey. We celebrate moments of deep personal insights into the subtleties of what it means to educate from the frame of reference that democracy is a moral way of living.

We conclude our preface with some final thoughts on the ecological characteristics of the fourfold process. Again, each fold is distinct but also inextricably connected to the others. You might be momentarily focused on creative teaching; but over time, you will recognize that these activities are not separate or isolated from the other three folds. In fact, as you gain experience with creative teaching, your sense of the other folds will undoubtedly deepen. And this will happen again and again as you gain experience with the other three folds. Generative lead-learning might crack open a deeper sense of professional awakening within you; or professional awakening may impact your thoughts and actions on the topics of participatory evaluating and creative teaching. And at any given point in your journey, you may be engaged in an interplay of all four folds.

Part of this feel for the ecological interdependence of the folds is acknowledging their fluid boundaries. Each fold overlaps and feeds into the others. Grab a piece of paper. Crumble it into a ball and then reopen it. Flatten out the paper ball and examine the folds that have been created. If you want, re-crumble the paper and reopen it. The folds you see and feel in the paper are always part of a network of other folds. And while each fold has boundaries, they collapse into each other again and again when the paper gets refolded. Taking this further, how one piece of paper folds is always different from another piece of paper. For example, a piece of butcher paper will fold and feel different than a piece of newsprint, construction paper, tissue paper, or cardstock. Likewise, your folded educational understandings will most likely be different in some small or large ways from the person right next to you or a person hundreds of miles away.

Another important insight into our fourfold process is the recognition that this problem solving is grounded in individuals mutually shaping and changing one another and their institutions. The fourfold process lives at the intersections of curriculum studies, teaching studies, and leadership studies. Because this book's problem solving is an amalgamation of these three disciplines, we can provide a quick summary of the process through the use of hyphens. Our four-fold process is an application of a particular *curriculum-teaching-leadership* conception. We don't treat curriculum, teaching, and leadership as isolated, compartmentalized endeavors; and by dissolving these three traditional disciplinary boundaries, we are theoretically leveling power hierarchies in education. We are not equating "leadership" with positional authority. Rather, our view is that regardless of one's job title, educators must share responsibilities when cultivating the artistry of teaching for subject understandings that are deepened through democratic self and social understandings.

We are not interested in theory for theory's sake; nor are we professing that once everyone acts in a certain prescribed way, an educational utopia will emerge. Such thinking is arguably fascistic, not democratic. We are not trying to convert you to our way of thinking. Rather, we are introducing an interpretation of educational problem solving that will, hopefully, inspire your educational imagination. Our presentation of the fourfold process is, ultimately, an invitation to pursue a particular type of professional excellence. We are hoping that our theoretical and practical guidance will encourage you to discover, or perhaps rediscover, your vocational calling to be an educator who is a lead professional for your society and its democratic aspirations.

In order to set the stage for the dance of ideas to come, we leave you with a table, "Key Features of the Fourfold Process," that highlights some of the distinct features of our fourfold process.

Key Features of the Fourfold Process

Professional Awakening	*Holistic Teaching*
• Rekindling a sense of vocational calling and agency in education • Refining historical and philosophical understandings of democratic education • Cultivating awareness of holistic education • Exploring your beliefs and images about the relationship between teaching, learning, curriculum, and leadership • Becoming a lead professional for democratic values • Establishing critical distance from: bureaucratic sleepwalking, professional isolation, and semi-professional habits	• Connecting your vocational journey to your students' vocational journeys • Finding imaginative ways to teach for subject understandings that are deepened by democratic self and social understandings • Reflecting on students' expressions of this holistic understanding • Facilitating students' journeys of understanding • Establishing critical distance from: adherence to predetermined teaching scripts, enforcement of passive information acquisition, and decontextualized rote instruction
Generative Lead-Learning	*Participatory Evaluating*
• Transacting meaningfully with colleagues on holistic pedagogy • Fostering an educational culture that honors and embraces disciplined study • Engaging in deliberative conversations on democratic education • Flattening management hierarchies • Creating supportive work cultures • Addressing needs or problems as a community • Recognizing that professionals don't grow in the same way • Affirming idiosyncratic journeys of personal-professional understanding • Establishing critical distance from authoritative, imposing, and manipulative actions that suppress journeys of understanding and promote management game playing and ethical sterility	• Generating authentic evaluation criteria • Transacting meaningfully on evaluative matters with students, colleagues, and other relevant curriculum stakeholders • Working with expressive outcomes and multiple forms of representation • Recognizing that a key purpose of evaluation is to educate and elevate pedagogical judgments and artistry in the interests of cultivating students' holistic understandings • Encouraging a relevant and meaningful diversity of evaluative interpretations • Establishing critical distance from management impositions and surveillance systems that do not allow for the emergence of pluralistic voices on what constitutes "good" education

Acknowledgments

Teaching is an intergenerational phenomenon, and each one of us stands on the shoulders of those who came before us. In turn, teachers become the shoulders on which future generations may choose to stand. We hope this book might be a humble contribution to the advancement of democratic curriculum and pedagogy in our current historical context with its pervasive standardized management policies in educational practice and narrow specializations in educational research. We want to acknowledge the open-hearted, broad-minded educators who have contributed to the creation of this book over twenty-seven years of action research. These professionals have actively worked with us to create a problem-solving approach that serves as a constructive alternative to restrictive accountability systems and narrow-minded scholarship. They have provided invaluable insights in how to best conceptualize a pragmatic, four-fold process that is grounded in democratic values.

Introduction

This book has been designed to provide educators and educational stakeholders—students, parents, local community leaders, political policymakers, and interested others—with guidance for the study and practice of a problem-solving process inspired by the great American philosopher, John Dewey. In a personal essay originally composed in 1897 and entitled *My Pedagogic Creed*, Dewey presents a concise statement of his educational philosophy which concludes with this assertion:

> Education . . . marks the most perfect and intimate union of science and art conceivable in human experience. The art of thus giving shape to human powers and adapting them to social service is the supreme art; one calling into its service the best of artists; that no insight, sympathy, tact, executive power, is too great for such service. Every teacher should realize the dignity of his [or her] calling; that he [or she] is a social servant set apart for the maintenance of proper social order and the securing of the right social growth. (Dewey, 2017, p. 40)

Dewey is asking his readers to envision education as a professional art that has a pivotal role in the advance of a powerful, value-based way of living in societies with democratic aspirations.

This book has been written with this historical and cultural vision in mind. How can educators incorporate a professional artistry into their daily curriculum, teaching, and leadership problem solving that advances democratic values? In more specific terms, this book is organized around the following four questions:

1. Why should educators pursue such a demanding professional purpose and social responsibility?

1

2. What is this problem-solving artistry?
3. How should educators build their capabilities to practice this problem-solving artistry?
4. How should this problem-solving artistry be evaluated?

PRESENTING SEVEN GUIDING PRINCIPLES

Seven principles of quality education guide the creation of this book's interpretation of problem-solving artistry. It shouldn't be surprising that these high-minded principles, which are informed by a diversified critical awareness, are both sophisticated and challenging; after all, they are inspired by Dewey's vision of education as a "supreme art." As briefly noted in the preface, the problem-solving artistry advanced in this text will be called *a fourfold process*. Following a presentation of the seven guiding principles, this chapter will conclude with a detailed introduction of the fourfold process.

Professional Responsibility

In 1916, Dewey composed an in-depth, definitive statement on his educational philosophy in a book titled *Democracy and Education*. In 2013, a leading contemporary educational philosopher, Nel Noddings, presented an update of Dewey's centerpiece text. In her book, titled *Education and Democracy in the 21st Century*, Noddings provides a concise philosophical platform for democratic teachers' vocational calling. Her accessible philosophical commentary is based on a critical distinction she makes between educational accountability and responsibility:

> Basic to accountability in any profession is the expectation that a practitioner should be able to *account for*, to justify, his or her professional decisions and acts. . . . Defining accountability entirely in terms of student test scores is a distortion of the concept. Even at its best, however, the concept of accountability has weaknesses. It puts too much emphasis on compliance, on answering to a higher authority. . . . *Responsibility* is a much more powerful concept for teachers. Whereas accountability points upward in the hierarchy and tends to direct teachers' attention to their own vulnerability for rewards or penalties, responsibility points downward in the chain of power to those dependent on our care and competence. (Noddings, 2013, p. 8)

This book presents a four-phased problem-solving process that is informed by Noddings's critical distinction between a semi-professional accountability that is enforced through standardized testing and a deep commitment to professional responsibility that is embodied in a caring competence.

Critical Pragmatism

The study and practice guidance that will be offered in this text is based on treating educators as thoughtful, disciplined critical thinkers engaged in socially responsible problem solving. Each problem-solving phase is an exercise in a particular type of critical thinking. Stated succinctly, this text is an application of the concept of critical pragmatism. As Cherryholmes (1988) notes, educators who practice critical pragmatism stand in contrast to educators who engage in a more vulgar, compliant, and value-free type of pragmatism. Critical pragmatists in education pose deep questions about the underlying values of educational policies and institutional structures. With respect to their institution's democratic mission statements, they openly and deeply question "official knowledge" (Apple, 1993). They are always on the alert for contradictions and hypocrisies—instances when educational words don't match educational actions. Cherryholmes (1988) argues that critical pragmatism is "based upon *visions* of what is beautiful, good, and true instead of fixed, structured, moral, or objective certainties. . . . Vulgar pragmatism . . . is pragmatism premised on unreflective acceptance of explicit and implicit standards, conventions, rules, and discourse-practices that we find around us" (p. 151). He then summarizes his distinction with this statement: "When being critical, one treats [habitual, customary] criteria and standards themselves as problematic" (p. 151). This book is guided by this important distinction between two fundamentally different approaches to pragmatic engagements.

Circuits of Valuation

Critical pragmatism is enacted through "circuits of valuation." Ryan (2011) explains this principle:

> I must ask myself whether what I like, desire, or value *really is* likable, desirable, or valuable. To determine this requires a test reflecting not just my present likes and dislikes, but the long-term interests of everyone affected by such an action, including myself. It requires, in other words, that a value candidate demonstrate its credentials as a genuine social value or good—not just a preference, but the end result of a process of valuation. (p. 66)

Ryan (2011) argues that modern societies around the world are currently experiencing a "crisis of modernity," which he summarizes as a broad cultural anxiety concerning the possibility of our "self-annihilation" should we fail to inquire into our values as we proceed with our decision-making: "We can't work together until we begin to *see* together—not some preconceived *what,* some universal good, but a common *how* that is experimental, inclusive, and pluralistic" (p. 76).

The four-phased process that will be presented in this text is a specific interpretation of Ryan's concept of "circuits of valuation." Ryan pictures such circuits as dynamic, recursive interplays between: (1) critiquing undemocratic habits and customs, (2) conceptualizing ways to address such critiques through proposed democratic values, (3) gaining experience with these value-based conceptions through trial-and-error practices, and (4) reviewing the enduring democratic impacts of these pragmatic actions (pp. 64–65). Circuits of valuation are practiced in an open-minded and humble way; the contrast to such problem solving would be actions that are based on the dogmatic, unquestioning assertion of values. With reference to Noddings's (2013) distinction between testing accountability and caring responsibility, the practice of circuits of valuation poses particular critical questions that have been incorporated into this book's practical advice chapters. Here's a sampling:

- What are the values that students are learning when testing surveillance systems are rigorously established, managed, and publicly recorded?
- How precisely are good test scores *valuable*?
- Do test-taking practices support and sustain undemocratic habits and customs?
- Are standardized tests the best way to encourage and advance students' democratic values? If not, what would be better ways to proceed?

These critical questions point to key organizing problem that this book is designed to address: how do educators become competent, lead professionals for problem-solving circuits that are guided by democratic values?

The Value of Pluralistic Humanism

Though there is an open set of democratic values that could inspire and inform this book's problem-solving approach depending on context and other deliberative contingencies, one particular value will be highlighted as a guiding principle. Due to its pivotal importance, pluralistic humanism stands out as a key moral consideration for the fourfold process. It is a complex value containing many subtleties. In his *Pedagogy of the Oppressed*, Freire (1971) argues for a consciousness-raising approach to adult literacy that he calls "conscientization." He writes, "By making it possible for men [and women] to enter the historical process as responsible subjects, conscientization enrolls them in the search for self-affirmation and thus avoids fanaticism" (p. 20). Freire is making the point that adults who learn to become historically aware agents feeling a sense of responsibility for their society's future become immune to narrow-minded, thoughtless, and scripted beliefs that are promulgated by doctrinaire ideologues. Freire's critical assertion is a central feature of liberal education rationales that trace back to the ancient Greeks. Null (2017) writes:

> Liberal education is an ideal that has shaped curriculum and teaching for centuries. . . . A liberating curriculum should turn students into free thinkers who can draw upon many fields of knowledge, pursue truth, and solve problems. To be free-minded means to use our minds to think independently while at the same time basing our judgments on a well-conceived view of tradition and purpose. . . . In a democratic state, a liberal curriculum should be offered to every citizen. (pp. 15–16)

In her analysis of liberal "consciousness" as an educational aim, the great American philosopher Maxine Greene (2017) argues that, "the 'work' with which we are here concerned is one of disclosure, reconstruction, generation. It is a work which culminates in a bringing something into being by the reader—in going beyond what he [or she] has been" (p. 149). Greene wants students to establish critical distance from narrow, dogmatic scripts through a personal embrace of pluralistic meaning making. She wants students to realize that, "what Schultz [1962] calls the attainment of a *'reciprocity of perspectives'* [is] the achievement of rationality. . . . 'To say there exists rationality,' writes Merleau-Ponty [1962], 'is to say that perspectives blend, perceptions confirm each other'" (p. 158).

Freire's, Null's, and Greene's arguments for pluralistic meaning making in education are augmented by a critical distinction that Merton (1997) makes between personalism and individualism:

> Personalism and individualism must not be confused. Personalism gives priority to the *person* and not the individual self. To give priority to the person means respecting the unique and inalienable value of the *other* person, as well as one's own, for a respect that is centered only on one's individual self to the exclusion of others proves itself to be fraudulent. (p. 17)

This pluralistic humanism—this valuing of others' diverse journeys of understanding as much as one values one's own journey of understanding—lies at the heart of democratic morality, and Garrison (1997) points out the importance of this principle for pragmatic problem solving:

> Finite creatures can grow wiser only if they share perspectives, for seeing things from the standpoint of others also allows us to multiply perspectives. That is why Dewey thought dialogues across differences were essential for those who desire to grow. When a single standpoint excludes others, the result is a distorted view of reality. Monism is dogmatism. (p. 15)

In this book, all forms of dogmatism are soundly rejected, and this rejection is informed by the interplay of the principles of pluralistic humanism and critical pragmatism.

Garrison is writing as a Western philosopher. The Eastern philosopher, Chuang Tzu, affirms the pragmatic nature of pluralistic humanism in more poetic terms: "The man in whom Tao acts without impediment harms no other being by his actions . . . He is not always looking for right and wrong . . . Great knowledge sees all in one. Small knowledge breaks down into the many" (Merton, 1997, pp. 40, 91). This possibility of generating great knowledge through a feel for the *one* in the *many* is insightfully examined by the French philosopher, Luc Ferry. He celebrates the pluralistic humanism embedded in the emergence of "singular" identities. Ferry (2005) writes:

> Singularities as transfigurations of particularities that are local in origin but bear a relationship to the universality of the world . . . defend a nondogmatic, nontribal, nonnationalistic conception of cultural identities that, although (or, rather, because) they are particular, enrich the world to which they are addressed and of which they are truly become a part as soon as they speak the language of the universal. From the viewpoint of the enlarged mentality, "shared culture" or "the sharing of cultures" enriches all of its components, not in the flat, demagogic sense of a mere respect for "folklore" or local artisanship," but in the more profound sense of the construction of a world that is at once diverse and held in common. This means that the notion of singularity can and must be directly attached to the ideal of that enlarged thought: when I broaden the scope of my experiences, I become singular, both because I surpass the particularity of my individual condition and because I accede, if not to universality, at least to an awareness that continually becomes more inclusive of, and richer in, the potentialities that are those of all humanity. (p. 282)

Ferry is arguing that singular "great knowledge" emerges out of the cultivation of pluralistic humanism, and there is a very basic way to understand this important insight. Practicing democratic morality requires a respectful pluralism; however, when this pluralism is not informed by a deep humanism, it can easily devolve into an undemocratic identity tribalism and politics. In parallel terms, practicing democratic morality requires a deep humanism; however, when this humanistic frame of reference is not guided by a respectful pluralism, it can easily devolve into an undemocratic liberal arts elitism that is insightfully critiqued in the post-humanism literature. Pluralistic humanism is an important principle to consider when practicing the fourfold process. The liberalized knowing that emerges out of this value orientation stands in vivid contrast to the narrow, compliant knowing promulgated by rigid, dehumanizing accountability systems.

Folding in Problem Solving

The four phases in the book's problem-solving process have no precise, step-by-step order. Studying and practicing this process is not like learning a technical procedure, such as acquiring competence with a software program. In this book, educators are being asked to embrace the complex, deliberative high ground that democratic morality requires. This requires them to critically question simplistic applications of technical rationality in education. There is certainly comfort in the acquisition of compact procedures, and such learning may have value in certain contexts. However, Gadamer's (1975) analysis of the synergy between humanistic truth and scientific method is a key guide for this book's fourfold process:

> What we mean by truth here can best be defined again in terms of our concept of *play*. The weight of things we encounter in understanding plays itself out in a linguistic event, a play of words playing around and about what is meant. *Language games* exist where we, as learners—and when do we cease to be that?—rise to the understanding of the world. . . . The certainty achieved by using scientific methods does not suffice to guarantee truth. This especially applies to the human sciences, but it does not mean that they are less scientific; on the contrary, it justifies the claim to special humane significance that they have always made. The fact that in such knowledge the knower's own being comes into play certainly shows the limits of method, but not of science. Rather, what the tool of method does not achieve must—and really can—be achieved by a discipline of questioning and inquiring, a discipline that guarantees truth. (pp. 483–84)

From the point of view of this book, following a precise procedure should never take the place of inquiring into the humanistic truths of democratic education. It is for this reason that—as explained in the preface—the four phases of this text's problem-solving approach are folded into one another in complex ways. Two metaphors might be helpful in further envisioning this principle. Imagine a satin sheet that is continuously folded and refolded in creative and fluid ways, generating static electricity as the folds rub against one another. This is how the dynamic spark of this book's problem-solving process is conceived. The philosopher, Gilles Deleuze, uses a paper metaphor to describe the complex "labyrinth" that results from folding processes:

> A continuous labyrinth is not a line dissolving into independent points, as flowing sand might dissolve into grains, but resembles a sheet of paper divided into infinite folds or separated into bending movements, each one determined by the consistent or conspiring surrounding. A fold is always folded within a fold, like a cavern in a cavern. (1992, p. 18)

The text's fourfold process approach is designed in a playful, nonlinear way; it is guided by the principle of folding in problem solving.

An Eclectic Approach to Curriculum, Teaching, and Leadership Studies

Advancing Dewey's vision of educational artistry requires the deconstruction of the academic, policy, and administrative boundaries between curriculum, teaching, and leadership which have become customary over a number of generations. Consequently, the creation of this text's fourfold process is guided by the principle of an eclectic integration of curriculum, teaching, and leadership studies. It is an application of Giroux's (1991) notion of "postmodern boundary crossing." In 1969, the curriculum theorist, Joseph Schwab, argued that since curriculum is a practical field, the "arts of the eclectic" are an essential feature of good curricular engagements. Schwab (2004) writes:

> All the social and behavioral sciences are marked by "schools," each distinguished by a different choice of principle of enquiry, each of which selects from the intimidating complexities of the subject matter the small fraction of the whole with which it can deal. The theories which arise from enquiries so directed are, then, radically incomplete. . . . It follows, then, that such theories are not, and will not be, adequate by themselves to tell us what to do with human beings or how to do it. What they variously suggest and the contrary guidances they afford to choice and action must be mediated and combined by eclectic arts. (p. 98)

This book's fourfold process is an application of an eclectic approach to the disciplines of curriculum, teaching, and leadership studies.

The Ethics of Democratic Practical Wisdom

Because the fourfold process is positioned in the deliberative middle ground of educational work, Aristotle's insights into the ethics of practical wisdom inform this book. In *Nicomachean Ethics*, Aristotle presents a set of moral and intellectual virtues that he views as central to the pursuit of human excellence, what the ancient Greeks called *arête*. For Aristotle, virtues are the ethical ways of knowing that result in admirable, inspired actions. Aristotle begins his analysis of virtues with a respectful nod to the technical artistry of crafts (*techné*) and concludes with a celebration of the holistic pleasure and happiness (*eudaimonia*) that wisdom brings to worthy, honorable living. He writes:

The intellect is the most excellent of the things in us, and the things with which the intellect is concerned are the most excellent of the things that can be known. Further, this [intellectual] activity is most continuous, for we are more able to contemplate continuously than we are to do anything else whatever. We also suppose that pleasure must be mixed into happiness, and the most pleasant of the activities in accord with virtue is agreed to be the one that pertains to wisdom. (2011, p. 224)

Roberts and Wood (2007) present a contemporary interpretation of Aristotle's ethics. They begin their discussion of the Aristotelian intellectual virtues with an analysis of the "love of knowledge" and conclude with an examination of "practical wisdom." They write: "Practical wisdom . . . is involved in every virtue, as constituting the good judgment without which no human virtue could be exemplified in action, emotion, or judgment. Insofar as virtues are human, they are infused with and qualified by reason, as the ancients would say; they are dispositions of intelligence" (p. 305). The advice in this book is guided by the recognition that practicing the fourfold process requires a commitment to a virtuous repertoire culminating in practical wisdom. We will have more to say about this topic in the next chapter.

Dewey's interpretation of freedom adds a contemporary, democratic perspective to Aristotle's ethical orientation. In his classic text on problem-solving excellence, titled *How We Think: A Restatement of the Relation of Reflective Thinking to the Educative Process*, Dewey (1933) defines freedom in this way:

Genuine freedom, in short, is intellectual; it rests in the trained power of thought, in ability to "turn things over," to look at matters deliberately, to judge whether the amount and kind of evidence requisite for decision is at hand, and if not, to tell where and how to seek such evidence. If a man's [or woman's] actions are not guided by thoughtful conclusions, then they are guided by inconsiderate impulse, unbalanced appetite, caprice, or the circumstances of the moment. To cultivate unhindered, unreflective external activity is to foster enslavement, for it leaves the person at the mercy of appetite, sense, and circumstance. (p. 90)

Dewey's interpretation of professional "freedom" as the practice of informed judgments is fundamental to this book's design. The focus of this book is on the advancement of democratic values in education; and through disciplined engagements in circuits of valuation, these values become embodied as democratic virtues. Due to the central importance of this topic, the challenges of cultivating a particular virtuous repertoire will be discussed in more detail in chapters 1 and 4.

INTRODUCING THE FOURFOLD PROCESS

The presentation of seven guiding principles sets the stage for an in-depth introduction of the fourfold process. In 1949, Ralph Tyler introduced his historically influential and paradigm setting "rationale" for good curriculum work in a book titled *Basic Principles of Curriculum and Instruction.* Because Tyler was working with a more conventional understanding of curriculum work, he could quickly introduce four sequential questions. He didn't need to introduce guiding principles. He quickly describes his four questions as problem-solving topics "which must be answered in developing any curriculum and plan of instruction" (p. 1). Tyler's questions are particular interpretations of four basic, interrelated curriculum concepts: purpose, experience, organization, and evaluation. The questions are presented in the following numbered sequence:

1. What educational **purposes** should the school seek to attain?
2. What educational **experiences** can be provided that are likely to attain these purposes?
3. How can these educational experiences be effectively **organized**?
4. How can we **[evaluate]** whether these purposes are being attained? (Tyler, 1949, p. 1)

The curriculum historian, Herbert Kliebard, provides guarded admiration of Tyler's problem-solving approach:

> One reason for the success of the Tyler rationale is its very rationality. It is an eminently reasonable framework for developing a curriculum; it duly compromises between warring extremes and skirts the pitfalls to which the doctrinaire are subject. In one sense the Tyler rationale is imperishable. (1992, p. 164)

This book's problem-solving approach builds on Kliebard's critical insight. There is definitely a non-doctrinaire and enduring inquiry logic underlying Tyler's way of integrating educational purposes with experience, organization, and evaluation. Unfortunately however, Tyler's rationale does not sufficiently defend against vulgar pragmatists who interpret this *purpose/experience/organization/evaluation* framework in reductionist, standardized, and top-down ways. This is mainly due to Tyler's emphasis in his rationale on the efficient clarification, organization, instruction, and evaluation of "behavioral objectives."

In our current historical era, the egregious example of such narrow, vulgar pragmatism would be policymakers who create doctrinaire management systems that enforce teaching for standardized test achievement. Such policymakers don't comprehend or appreciate the purposing, teaching, capacity building, and evaluating that will be advanced in this book. Compare Tyler's four sequential questions to the questions guiding this book's fourfold process:

1. **Professional Awakening**: How are we awakening to a professionally compelling, holistic interpretation of educational purpose?
2. **Holistic Teaching**: How are we experiencing the transactional artistry of teaching for students' subject understandings deepened by democratic self and social understandings?
3. **Generative Lead-Learning**: How are we reorganizing for an authentic culture that nurtures the capacity-building that this pedagogical artistry requires?
4. **Participatory Evaluating**: How are we democratically reviewing the diversified expressive outcomes and social impacts of this pedagogical artistry?

The next chapter will provide an in-depth theoretical explanation of this fourfold process, and the following four chapters will provide practical guidance on the enactment of this process as a particular circuit of democratic valuation. The following chart, which is organized around Tyler's *purpose/ experience/organization/evaluation* framework, provides an overview of the key critical contrasts informing this book's fourfold process.

The organizing questions for this book's fourfold process are all phrased with the collaborative and inclusive "we" pronoun. By contrast, notice how the first question in Tyler's sequential process uses an impersonal institutional referent: "school." But who is speaking for the school? Tyler's rationale remains vague about this important matter, and this is particularly relevant since he uses the pronoun "we" in the last question in his four-step sequence. Who is the "we" that decides on the designated educational purposes and whether or not such purposes have been achieved? Who exercises this evaluative power? Is it teachers, students' parents, educational administrators, community leaders, state bureaucrats, politicians, policymakers, some other group, or some combination of these stakeholders? *Most importantly for this book, will the evaluative power that is conceived and exercised advance enduring democratic values?* Because it is not grounded in critical pragmatism, Tyler's problem-solving approach does not address this fundamental question.

When Tyler published his *Basic Principles of Curriculum and Instruction* text in 1949, Dewey was still alive. In fact, Dewey published his final co-authored book, titled *Knowing and the Known*, in 1949. Tyler was certainly aware of Dewey's 1897 vision of education as a democratically aspiring society's pivotal professional art, so why didn't he build that vision into his first question concerning educational purposes? Why is Tyler so vague about

Democratic Lead Learning

Tyler's Framework	*Tyler's Rationale*	*Accountability Compliance*	*The Book's Fourfold Process*
Purpose	Clearly Stating Educational Objectives	Establishing Publicly Mandated, Systematic Metrics	Professional Awakening: Becoming a Lead Professional for Democratic Values
Experience	Selecting Useful Learning Experiences for the Objectives	Preparing for the Efficient Transmission of Knowledge for Test-taking Achievement	Holistic Teaching: Practicing Holistic Pedagogical Transactions
Organization	Organizing Learning Experiences into Effective Instructional Units, Courses, and Programs	Creating Curriculum Maps for Continuous Standardized Test Improvement	Generative Lead-Learning: Building the Necessary Repertoires for the Creative Teaching
Evaluation	Determining the Effectiveness of the Learning Experiences in Attaining the Specified Objectives	Measuring, Recording, and Reporting the Common Assessments	Participatory Evaluating: Democratically Reviewing Expressive Outcomes and Social Impacts

this important matter? This book's problem-solving approach stands in vivid contrast to Tyler's rationale precisely because these two critical questions are clearly and unequivocally addressed in ways that are compatible with generative "power with" (Kreisberg, 1992) and "power within" (Henderson, 2010; Henderson et al., 2015) frames of reference.

There is a reason this introductory chapter begins with a quote from Dewey's 1897 educational vision. The text's fourfold process is organized around the fundamental idea that when education is interpreted as a pivotal professional art steeped in democratic values, a particular type of power-with and power-within leadership is required. This collaborative leadership is framed as "lead learning" by the leadership studies scholar, Roland Barth. Barth (2008) writes, "In our [education] profession, especially, one [who] is a learner . . . [is] THEREBY a leader. The moral authority of the educational leader comes first and foremost from being a learner" (p. x). Foster (1989) clarifies Barth's interpretation of the moral authority of educational leaders in the following way:

Leadership, in the final analysis, is the ability of humans to relate deeply to each other in the search for a more perfect union. Leadership is a consensual task, a sharing of ideas and a sharing of responsibilities, where a "leader" is a leader for the moment only, where the leadership exerted must be validated by the consent of followers, and where leadership lies in the struggles of a community to find meaning for itself. (p. 61)

Foster's collaborative, community-based sense of educational leadership goes to the heart of our understanding of generative lead-learning.

Imagine the societal impact of thousands of highly motivated lead-learning educators engaging in this text's fourfold process as they go about their daily lesson planning, student-centered teaching, collegial communicating, program developing, and a host of other educational activities. What would be the cultural ripple effects of their collaborative work on their society's critical awareness and democratic values? In his masterful book on educational imagination, Eisner (1994) writes:

School reform efforts have typically focused on single-shot panaceas: flexible scheduling, educational accountability . . . site-based management, voucher programs. None of these single-shot efforts have had or are likely to have a major impact on the character of schools. . . . To create schools that genuinely educate . . . [leaders] must pay attention to the deep aims of the enterprise, to the structure that schools possess, to the curriculum that they offer, to the quality of teaching that occurs, and to the forms of evaluation and assessment that are employed to understand its consequences. (p. 383)

Eisner's vision of educational reform informs this book, and his argument for a comprehensive approach to leadership informs this text's fourfold process.

The practice of the fourfold process raises the question of inspired professional development. The current state of authentic democratic aspirations in education is decidedly uneven and conflicted. How many educators, particularly those with positional authority, embody the ethical fidelity that they espouse? Badiou (2001) defines ethical fidelity as a faithful and humble commitment to "matters of human rights and humanitarian actions" (p. 10). With reference to his interpretation of ethical fidelity, how many educators honestly and persistently "walk" their democratic talk? How many of them open-heartedly practice what they rhetorically preach?

As already noted, Tyler's problem-solving "rationale" can easily be adapted for the purpose of implementing a power-over surveillance system.[1] This is not the case with this book's fourfold process. It cannot be used for top-down enforcement purposes because it draws its sense of fidelity from educators' vocational callings—from the thoughts, feelings, and beliefs that inspired them to be educators committed to holistic, democratic education.

The book's fourfold process can be practiced in any educational setting, though perhaps only on a small scale where there is "wiggle room" in systems enforcing the standardized management of teachers (Cuban, 2003). Without institutional support, the text's lead-learning approach may need to be practiced informally by a small group of interested educators—perhaps by only two professional partners acting as critical friends. The problem-solving advice offered in this book is based on the critical recognition that not all educators are ready to embrace the developmental challenges embedded in a fourfold process grounded in a visionary, holistic, collaborative, and deliberative discipline. Lead learners may plant seeds, but those seeds may never grow or only grow after lying dormant for many years. Nonetheless, there are a sizable number of dedicated, persevering seed-planters in the education profession. We know from experience that many educators feel the powerful call to the vibrancy and virtues of teaching that is grounded in democratic values. We feel there is much hope for this book's problem-solving advocacy.

THE BOOK'S ORGANIZATION

As we have already mentioned, the recommendations for the disciplined study and practice of this book's problem-solving approach will be presented in a personal and inviting writing style. We—the three co-authors of this book—are practicing teachers, and we begin our guidance with a theoretical platform that is crafted as a collegial conversation. The fourfold process we are advancing is based on a particular theoretical orientation, and we feel that understanding this orientation is a professionally and politically important step for motivated and motivating educators. Educators must be able to critically explain and justify this book's problem-solving approach to a broad range of curriculum stakeholders, including policymakers, community leaders, and parents. The discussion of our theoretical platform will be followed by illustrated guidance on the study and practice of each fold, and our advice will be offered in an open-ended montage format. As mentioned in the preface, each montage is a diverse collection of inquiry prompts, supportive quotations, critical commentaries, practical tips, narrative illustrations, and continuing study recommendations. Though we have created four discrete montages, we will continuously emphasize the recursive and iterative interweaving of the four folds.

We then conclude the book in our epilogue by affirming and celebrating the personal-professional journeying that is embedded in our problem-solving guidance. We present an ethical code that was created by an Ohio teacher leader who has been introduced to the study and practice of the fourfold process. This experienced teacher used the Hippocratic Oath in the medical professions as a referent for creating a guiding ethical "covenant." We believe this is a fitting way to end a text that introduces a carefully researched, pragmatic interpretation of Dewey's vision of educational artistry in societies with democratic aspirations.

NOTE

1. Hlebowitsh (1993) argues that it was not Tyler's intention to promote the management of teachers. Given the complete arc of Tyler's career, this is probably the case. Perhaps Tyler's inattention to the distinction between critical and vulgar pragmatism is not so much a personal limitation but an artifact of the academic culture of his generation of curriculum scholars. In short, Tyler's lack of critical awareness may mainly be traced to habit and custom.

REFERENCES

Apple, M. W. (1993). *Official knowledge: Democratic education in a conservative age.* New York, NY: Routledge.

Aristotle. (2011). *Aristotle's Nicomachean ethics.* (R. C. Bartlett & S. D. Collins, Trans.). Chicago, IL: University of Chicago Press.

Badiou, A. (2001). *Ethics: An essay on the understanding of evil.* (P. Hallward, Trans.). London: Verso.

Barth, R. S. (2008). Foreword. In G. A. Donaldson, *How leaders learn: Cultivating capacities for school improvement* (pp. ix–xi). New York, NY: Teachers College Press.

Cherryholmes, C. H. (1988). *Power and criticism: Poststructural investigations in education.* New York, NY: Teachers College Press.

Cuban, L. (2003). *Why is it so hard to get good schools?* New York, NY: Teachers College Press.

Deleuze, G. (1992). *The fold: Leibniz and the baroque.* Minneapolis, MN: University of Minnesota Press.

Dewey, J. (1916). *Democracy and education.* New York, NY: Macmillan.

———. (1933). *How we think: A restatement of the relation of reflective thinking to the educative process.* Boston, MA: D.C. Heath & Company. (Original work published 1910)

———. (2017). My pedagogic creed. In D. J. Flinders & S. J. Thornton (Eds.), *The curriculum studies reader* (5th ed., pp. 33–40). New York, NY: Routledge. (Original work published 1897)

Dewey, J., & Bentley, A. F. (1949). *Knowing and the known.* Boston, MA: Beacon Press.

Eisner, E. W. (1994). *The educational imagination: On the design and evaluation of school programs* (3rd ed.). New York, NY: Macmillan.

Ferry, L. (2005). *What is the good life?* (L. G. Cochrane, Trans.). Chicago, IL: University of Chicago Press.

Foster, W. (1989). Toward a critical practice of leadership. In J. Smyth (Ed.), *Critical Perspectives on Educational Leadership* (pp. 39–62). New York, NY: Routledge-Falmer.

Freire, P. (1971). *Pedagogy of the oppressed*. New York, NY: Herder and Herder.

Gadamer, H. G. (1975). *Truth and method*. (G. Barden & J. Cumming, Eds. & Trans.). New York, NY: Seabury.

Garrison, J. (1997). *Dewey and eros: Wisdom and desire in the art of teaching*. New York, NY: Teachers College Press.

Greene, M. (2017). Curriculum and consciousness. In D. J. Flinders & S. J. Thornton (Eds.), *The curriculum studies reader* (5th ed., pp. 147–59). New York, NY: Routledge. (Original work published 1971)

Giroux, H. A. (1991). *Postmodernism, feminism, and cultural politics: Redrawing educational boundaries*. Albany, NY: State University of New York Press.

Henderson, J. G. (2010). *The path less taken: Immanent critique in curriculum and pedagogy*. J. L. Schneider (Ed.). New York, NY: Educator's International Press.

Henderson, J. G., et al. (2015). *Reconceptualizing curriculum development: Inspiring and informing action*. New York, NY: Routledge.

Hlebowitsh, P. (1993). *Radical curriculum theory reconsidered: A historical approach*. New York, NY: Teachers College Press.

Kliebard, H. M. (1992). *Forging the American curriculum: Essays in curriculum history and theory*. New York, NY: Routledge.

Kreisberg, S. (1992). *Transforming power: Domination, empowerment, and education*. Albany, NY: State University of New York Press.

Merleau-Ponty, M. (1962). *Phenomenology of perception*. (D. A. Landis, Trans.). London: Routledge Kegan Paul.

Merton, T. (1997). *The way of Chuang Tzu*. New York, NY: New Directions Books.

Noddings, N. (2013). *Education and democracy in the 21st century*. New York, NY: Teachers College Press.

Null, W. (2017). *Curriculum: From theory to practice* (2nd ed.). Lanham, MD: Rowman & Littlefield.

Roberts, R. C., & Wood, W. J. (2007). *Intellectual virtues: An essay in regulative epistemology*. New York, NY: Clarendon Press.

Ryan, F. X. (2011). *Seeing together: Mind, matter and the experimental outlook of John Dewey and Arthur F. Bentley*. Great Barrington, MA: American Institute for Economic Research.

Schultz, A. (1962). *Collected papers I, The problem of social reality*. M. A. Natanson & H. L. van Breda (Eds.). Dordrecht, The Netherlands: Martinus Nijhoff.

Schwab, J. J. (2004). The practical: A language for curriculum. In D. J. Flinders & S. J. Thornton (Eds.), *The curriculum studies reader* (2nd ed., pp. 103–17). New York, NY: Routledge. (Original work published 1969)

Tyler, R. W. (1949). *Basic principles of curriculum and instruction*. Chicago, IL: University of Chicago Press.

Chapter One

Theoretical Platform

OPENING COMMENTS

Our theoretical platform serves as the starting point for the montage guidance on the study and practice of the fourfold process that we will be presenting in chapters 2–5. We could call this platform a framework or rationale, but there is a particular professional reason we have chosen the "platform" term. In 1971, Decker Walker published an important research article documenting how educators practiced curriculum problem solving when they were not subjected to top-down management pressures. Walker (1971) coined the term, "naturalistic curriculum development," to describe this professional awareness and assertiveness. Thirty-eight years later, Walker and Soltis (2009) provide this concise summary of naturalistic curriculum development:

> In studying how curriculum development groups actually worked, Walker found that . . . their starting point appeared to be a set of *beliefs* and *images* they shared—beliefs about the content; about the students, their needs, and how they learn; about schools, classrooms, and teaching; about the society and its needs; and images of good teaching, of good examples of content and method, and of good procedures to follow. They spent a great deal of time stating and refining these beliefs [and images], which comprised what Walker called their "platform." (p. 62)

The montage guidance that we have created for this book is based on a particular theoretical platform; it is a coherent articulation of our beliefs and images of what constitutes educational artistry in societies with democratic aspirations. It provides a deliberative rationale for our four study-and-practice montages, and our justification for the relevance of the fourfold process. To summarize, we think that providing such a theoretical argument is a professionally responsible step to take at the onset of this book. Let us explain.

We agree with Schubert's (1986) statement that, "When fundamental curriculum questions are not addressed by educators, economic or political caprice leads the way and educational practice is governed by default" (p. 1). Dewey (1938) attributes such a default position in education to a reliance on habit and custom instead of thoughtful inquiry. When educational activities are not based on critically informed judgments, they are not professional. Such activities are, essentially, behavioral manifestations of a compliant semi-professionalism. When teachers are required to "teach-to-the-test" to demonstrate their "fidelity" to institutional mandates, particularly when their judgments tell them that they should be working otherwise with their students, they are not practicing professional responsibility as described by Noddings (2013) in our introduction. We think this is unfortunate. We think top-down, standardized management policies result in positioning educators as narrow technicians and test proctors, not as thoughtful professionals.

Dewey (1933) describes three "attitudes" that he thinks are essential for problem-solving artistry in education: open-mindedness, whole-heartedness, and responsibility. Open-minded problem solvers are careful to avoid narrow prejudice and rigid partisanship. They become whole-heartedly absorbed by the problem, enthusiastically and open-mindedly studying all of its holistic subtleties. As Dewey notes, "When a person is absorbed, the subject carries him [or her] on . . . further inquiries and readings are indicated and followed" (p. 31). This open-mindedness and whole-heartedness sets the stage for a sense of responsibility elegantly summarized by Dewey:

> To be intellectually responsible is to consider the consequences of a projected step; it means to be willing to adopt these consequences when they follow reasonably from any position already taken. Intellectual responsibility secures integrity; that is to say, consistency and harmony in belief. (p. 32)

Our montage guidance is designed to promote this sense of study-based, intellectual responsibility.

In his review of the foundations of comprehensive and holistic evaluation, Schwandt (2015) argues that professional educational judgments require "preparation in theoretical knowledge and practical reason" (p. 147). Our montage advice is based on recognizing the importance of this theory-practice balance. Schwandt concludes his argument by listing five "qualities [that] make for sustainable, lifelong growth in professional competence and commitment" (p. 147). These five professional developmental qualities were identified by the Carnegie Foundation for the Advancement of Teaching as a guide for their "Preparation for the Professions Program." We quote two of these Carnegie Foundation qualities because they are particularly relevant to the construction of our theoretical platform:

- Deep engagement with the profession's public purposes, along with a sense of meaning and satisfaction from one's work that is grounded in or aligned with those purposes.
- The capacity and inclination to contribute to the ethical quality of the profession and its institutions. This includes a sense of moral agency in relation to morally questionable aspects of the institutional context, and the moral imagination and courage to create more constructive institutional structures or practices (Colby & Sullivan, 2008, p. 415).

There is one final preliminary point we wish to make before presenting our theoretical platform; and in many ways, it is central to our justifications. *We believe in the power of a hermeneutic humility that is grounded in disciplined study and critical fluidity.* The term, hermeneutics, is derived from the Greek god, Hermes, who served as the messenger between the diverse pantheon of gods in Olympus and humans seeking wisdom. Hermeneutics—in all of its religious, legal, and philosophical manifestations—involves the arts of interpreting the nuanced complexities of some matter as a guide for practical reasoning. For example, the Supreme Court justices in the United States have the final hermeneutic responsibility of translating the complex intricacies of power and justice in the American Constitution into workable principles for the legal professions. In short, their job is to clearly communicate how a "network" (Greene, 2017) of democratic meanings, perspectives, and pronouncements can be a useful guide for judicial practices.

As we have noted, Dewey felt that deliberating over many possible interpretations of some educational matter before making a practical judgment involves open-minded, open-hearted, and responsible engagements. The philosopher, Hans-Georg Gadamer (1975) characterizes such deliberation as an exercise in "dialogical play." He argues that there is a truth-seeking humility that is embedded in such conversational playfulness with its commitment to thoughtfully broadening one's "horizons," and such hermeneutic humility stands in contrast to the human arrogance and black-and-white thinking that are features of all forms of literalism, fundamentalism, and authoritarianism.

Pinar, Reynolds, Slattery, and Taubman (1995) argue that curriculum must be hermeneutically understood as engagements in "complicated conversation." They write: "Curriculum is intensely historical, political, racial, gendered, phenomenological, autobiographical, aesthetic, theological and international. Curriculum becomes the site on which the generations struggle to define themselves and the world. Curriculum is an extraordinarily complicated conversation" (pp. 847–48). Our theoretical platform is based on this hermeneutic embrace of curriculum complexity. As we will shortly discuss in more detail, we believe in the importance of integrating such complicated curriculum conversations into teaching deliberations. In short, we recognize the vital importance of deliberative artistry in education.

Such educational deliberations are nurtured by disciplined study. William Pinar's work on understanding the nuanced complexities of curriculum sparked the "reconceptualization" of curriculum studies, which he summarizes as a refocusing away from narrow empirical research agendas to a broad "rethinking of the basic concepts of the field" (Pinar, 2000, pp. x–xi). In a book subtitled, "Curriculum Development after the Reconceptualization," Pinar (2006) argues that disciplined study should be the heart and soul of curriculum development after the reconceptualization of the field. Citing Robert McClintock's 1971 essay on the topic of disciplined study, Pinar (2006) writes:

> Study is the site of education. Not instruction, not learning, but study constitutes the process of education, a view, McClintock tells us, [that is] grounded in "individuality," "autonomy," and "creativity." McClintock . . . emphasizes the significance of our "particularity," that we become more that we have been influenced to be, that we . . . refashion ourselves by engaging "freely" and "creatively" with our circumstances. . . . Study is a spiritual discipline. It is an intellectual discipline as well. . . . Schwab's [1978] notion of "deliberation" [fosters] complicated conversation [that] is simultaneously intellectual and spiritual. . . . Study is not theoretical but practical, not reverential but critical. (pp. 112–14)

We have created our montage guidance with this nuanced understanding of disciplined curriculum studies in mind. Our fourfold process is designed to advance a study-based lead-learning that fosters individuality, autonomy, and creativity. We will have more to say about the personal, generative nature of this interpretation of collaborative leadership when we discuss the third fold in the process.

As we noted in the preface and introductory chapter, our fourfold process with its guiding principles is built on a diversified critical awareness. Consequently, it shouldn't be surprising that a "critical itineracy" (Paraskeva, 2016)—a dynamic critical movement across all four folds—is built into our montage guidance. This is a conceptual "traveling" that rejects ideological rigidity, and our fluid approach to critical theorizing is insightfully analyzed and advocated by the curriculum scholar, Marla Morris. In her two-volume guidebook, she writes that "the student of curriculum studies is a traveler . . . , [so] travel is an apt metaphor for a field that is in flux . . . [and] is vast . . . " (Morris, 2016, pp. 1–2). To summarize, we recognize that the problem solving we are advancing has many moving parts involving a subtle, study-based journey of understanding. The professional excellence we are advancing cannot be quickly achieved.

THEORETICAL PLATFORM

Based on twenty-seven years of action research in the context of three major transformative curriculum leadership and teacher leadership grants, as well as two Kent State University graduate courses (Fundamentals of Curriculum and Curriculum Leadership), we believe that teaching for a particular holistic understanding is a compelling way to interpret John Dewey's 1897 vision of education, which we cited in the introductory chapter's opening paragraph, as the "supreme" professional art in societies with democratic aspirations. The holistic pedagogy we have in mind is teaching for *S*ubject understandings that are deepened by democratic *S*elf and *S*ocial understandings. For shorthand purposes, we call this purposeful teaching, 3S pedagogy.

The concept of 3S pedagogy is informed by Kirylo's (2016) insightful analysis of "teaching with purpose." He begins his concluding chapter with a quote from Dewey's *The School and Society:* "What the best and wisest parent wants for his own child, that must the community want for all of its children. Any other ideal for our schools is narrow and unlovely; and acted upon, it destroys our democracy" (1943, pp. 6–7). Recognizing the comprehensive, holistic, and collaborative nature of such democratic teaching, Kirylo concludes his book with this statement:

> For teachers who authentically understand the who and why they teach; who are contextually aware; who are clear about the critical aspects of teaching, and think globally, but act locally, the entire community will radiate toward the direction of purposeful educational transformation. (p. 160)

From a problem-solving standpoint, we recognize that our 3S pedagogical interpretation of Dewey's 1897 vision is a hypothesis embedded in the logic of pragmatic inquiry with its emphasis on learning through experience. Our four-phased process is a specific articulation of this educational logic. We recognize that these four phases are folded into one another in complicated ways. Therefore, as we noted in our preface and introductory chapter, we describe the problem solving as a *fourfold process* with each fold having a particular organizing *term* and *question*. Here, again, are our four terms and questions:

• *Professional Awakening*: How are we awakening to a professionally compelling, holistic interpretation of educational purpose?

- *Holistic Teaching*: How are we experiencing the transactional artistry of teaching for students' subject understandings deepened by democratic self and social understandings?
- *Generative Lead-Learning*: How are we reorganizing for an authentic culture that nurtures the capacity building that this pedagogical artistry requires?
- *Participatory Evaluating*: How are we democratically reviewing the diversified expressive outcomes and impacts of this pedagogical artistry?

Our theoretical platform is an explanation of why we chose these particular organizing terms and questions. The four montage chapters that follow our platform presentation will provide detailed practical guidance on how to understand these concepts and pursue these questions through disciplined study and practice.

First Fold: Professional Awakening

We describe our first fold as "professional awakening." There are two reasons why we don't just refer to this problem solving as pursuing specific educational goals. First, we want to make a clear critical distinction between managing educators as semi-professionals and supporting educators as professional artists. Both semi-professional and professional educators have goals; but there is an important qualitative difference in the purposefulness of the two groups. We want to unequivocally and explicitly signal the professionalization that is built into our fourfold process. Second, our research on this process has clearly documented the critical awakening that results from the study and practice of our process (Henderson & Gornik, 2007; Henderson et al., 2015), and this should not be surprising. If teachers tend to teach as they were taught (Lortie, 1975); and if they are primarily taught by managed, semi-professional educators, it shouldn't be unexpected that they would experience our problem-solving approach as a critical awakening.

We use "compelling" in this fold's organizing question to recognize that the fourfold process is invitational. We want to establish critical distance from management imposition and surveillance and clearly acknowledge the motivational foundations of our problem-solving approach. Pink (2009) organizes his analysis of adult intrinsic motivation into three interrelated categories: purpose, autonomy and mastery, and he summarized the interplay of these three motivational themes as follows:

> We know that the richest experiences in our lives aren't when we're clamoring for validation from others, but when we are listening to our own voice—doing something that matters, doing it well, and doing it in the service of a cause larger than ourselves. (p. 145)

Pink celebrates the authentic freedom that comes with this sense of existential, visionary purpose: "We're born to be players, not pawns. We're meant to be autonomous individuals, not individual automatons" (p. 106). He concludes his analysis by noting that this quest for personal mastery requires a commitment to disciplined learning, to the enjoyment of developmental pursuits, and to a balancing of work and play (pp. 118–28).

We think Pink's analysis captures the subtleties of the vocational calling that our fourfold process encourages. When educators are introduced to 3S pedagogy as a particular holistic interpretation of Dewey's 1897 vision of educational artistry, they become immediately aware of the motivational and developmental challenges associated with this teaching practice. They can clearly see that they are being invited to pursue a type of professional excellence that rises above the customary view of teaching as a relatively simple-minded technical craft. They quickly recognize that the cultivation of 3S pedagogical artistry involves a disciplined journey of understanding, which challenges them to ponder if they are ready for such a long-term undertaking.

Second Fold: Holistic Teaching

This motivational and developmental feature of our problem-solving approach not only applies to teachers, it also applies to their students, and this is an important matter in the conceptualization of the second "holistic teaching" fold. There is a transactional relationship between teachers' professional journeys of understanding and their students' holistic journeys of 3S understandings. In short, teachers' 3S pedagogical development and students' holistic development are intimately bound together. Consequently, 3S pedagogy is both teacher-centered and student-centered. Teachers gain experience with 3S pedagogical artistry by providing their students with educational experiences that foster their 3S understanding. 3S pedagogy involves transactional learning involving both a teacher's and his/her students' holistic journeys.

Near the end of his career and life, Dewey came to the conclusion that "transaction" was a better term for his understanding of educational experience, and Dewey's philosophical explanation of the transactional concept was clarified in his last co-authored book, *Knowing and the Known*. Ryan (2011) explains Dewey's insight that transactional relations are at the heart of educational experience:

> Transactional relations offer a more broadly human view of scientific practices than the reduction of reality to fixed laws and interacting particles. Quantum physics offers breathtaking insights, but it doesn't reduce reality to particles and forces. Instead, it binds the reality of what we discover to the reality of our expanding pursuits and interests. Where reductionism looks for a single point

on the continuum marking ultimate reality, transaction finds reality abundant in
each phase of an expanding range of relationships. (p. 47)

Our organizing question for "holistic teaching" includes the idea of "transactional artistry" for a key reason. We want to make a clear critical distinction
between forms of management reductionism—such as defining "quality"
education through standardized test measurements—and the practice of 3S
pedagogical artistry. A holistic, transactional "power-with" is a central feature of 3S pedagogy.

Eisner's (1994b) analysis of the "art of teaching" provides important critical
insights into the challenges of 3S pedagogical artistry. He describes four ways to
understand creative teaching. Such teachers work with an aesthetic feel for the
transactional moments in lessons, and he notes that "we use the adjectives and
accolades usually applied to the fine arts to describe [such pedagogy]" (p. 155).
This mindful teaching requires "judgments based largely on qualities that unfold
during the course of action" (p. 155), and practicing such qualitative judgments
is characteristic of all forms of art. These judgments involve inventive "ingenu-
ity" and an attentive openness to "emergent" ends. He writes: "Teaching is a
form of human action in which many of the ends achieved are . . . found in the
course of interaction with students rather than preconceived and efficiently attained" (p. 155). Eisner (1994b) concludes his analysis of pedagogical artistry by
stating that "teaching . . . is sensitive, intelligent, and creative—those qualities
that confer on it the status of an art. . . . It should, in my view, not be regarded as
it so often is by some, as an expression of unfathomable talent or luck but as an
example of humans exercising the highest levels of their intelligence" (p. 156).

3S pedagogy involves a transactional vocational artistry: the art of this
holistic teaching is focused on the emergence of students' future vocational
artistries. As students work on their subject understandings deepened by
democratic self and social understandings, they are positioning themselves
for the artistry of their vocational pursuits. Drawing on the work of Sir Herbert Read, Eisner (2005) explains:

Sir Herbert Read, an English art historian, poet, and pacifist working during
the middle of the last century . . . and I concur that the aim of education ought
to be conceived as the preparation of artists. By the term "artist," neither he
nor I mean necessarily painters and dancers, poets and playwrights. We mean
individuals who have developed the ideas, the sensibilities, the skills, and the
imagination to create work that is well proportioned, skillfully executed, and
imaginative, regardless of the domain in which an individual works. The highest accolade we can confer upon someone is to say that he or she is an artist,
whether as a carpenter or a surgeon, a cook or an engineer, a physicist or a
teacher. The fine arts have no monopoly on the artistic. (p. 208)

As co-authors of this book, we strongly embrace Dewey's (1958) view of "art as experience." We imagine teachers working with a deeply generous and generative "perception" of human excellence, and we critically challenge educational policies, structures, and practices that promote mediocrity.

We imagine a critical mass of future teachers who are passionately pursuing a vocational artistry that invites and fosters students' personal pursuits of their vocational artistries. In 1896, Dewey created a laboratory school at the University of Chicago to demonstrate his educational philosophy. He summarizes the key curricular problem in his school's teaching practices as follows:

> The pressing problem with respect to "subject matter" was accordingly to find those things in the direct present experience of the young which were roots out of which would grow more elaborate . . . organized knowledge in later years. . . . The solution of the problem . . . is the discovery of those things which are genuinely personal experiences, but which lead out into the future and into a wider and more controlled range of interests and purposes. This was the problem of subject matter to which the school was devoted. (Dewey, 1966, pp. 468–69)

Dewey's analysis of the "problem" of subject matter instruction is interpreted in this book as the challenge of teaching for subject matter understandings that are deepened by democratic self and social understandings. In short, teaching for *3S* understanding.

Third Fold: Generative Lead-Learning

The possible emergence of such a critical mass of educators who are dedicated to cultivating their 3S pedagogical artistry will require an authentic cultural support that is generally not a feature of current educational organizations. A reorganizing effort must be undertaken, which brings us to the third fold in the problem-solving process. Our descriptive term and organizing question for this fold requires some detailed explanation. As discussed in the introductory chapter, democratic lead-learning is one of the fundamentals guiding the creation of the fourfold process. Democracy is a collaborative, power-with phenomenon. As Dewey and many other philosophers note, one of the benefits of democratic living is a disciplined and generous tolerance for different perspectives. Such respectful "dissensus" (Nancy, 2000; Rancière, 2010), which stands in contrast to debilitating and destructive dissensus, can foster a deepening humanism. This is a guiding principle in healthy scientific communities with their constructive commitments to the pragmatic advancement of knowledge. Abraham Lincoln, who is arguably America's greatest president, practiced such pragmatism on a broad political scale during the United States' civil war crisis, and his commitment to respectful dissensus is carefully documented in Doris Kearns Goodwin's (2005) *Team of Rivals: The Political Genius of Abraham Lincoln.*

We refer to generative lead-learning with this constructive dissensus in mind, and we recognize the humility that is embedded in this interpretation of educational leadership. Educators, particularly teachers, who take the lead in the study and practice of the fourfold process, can be authentically humble in their quest for professional excellence. As generative lead-learners, they can honestly state that they are not experts in 3S pedagogical artistry, they are simply pursuing a demanding developmental commitment and would love to have some collaborative companionship along the way. In fact, they can note that such study-based, respectful reciprocity will prove to be mutually beneficial.

The sense of reciprocity is a central feature in Maxine Greene's interpretation of human freedom. In *The Dialectic of Freedom*, she states that when oppression or exploitation is seen as "natural" or "given," the notion of human freedom can feel quite remote: "A teacher in search of his/her own freedom may be the only kind of teacher who can arouse young persons to go in search of their own" (p. 14). She critically describes the human struggles to be "free from" limitations, oppression, alienation, and coercion so as to experience the "freedom to" come together as authentic individuals around projects everyone can mutually pursue: "Negative freedom is the right not to be interfered with or coerced or compelled to do what they did not choose to do" (p.16). She celebrates narratives of "positive freedom . . . [which] articulate connections between the individual search for freedom and appearing before others in an open place, a public and political sphere" (p. 116). Her analysis of this negative/positive dialectic of freedom includes the following vision of educational emancipation:

> This is what we shall look for as we move: freedom developed by human beings who have acted to make a space for themselves in the presence of others. Human beings become "challengers" ready for alternatives, alternatives that include caring and community. And we shall seek, as we go, implications for emancipatory education conducted by and for those willing to take responsibility for themselves and for each other. We want to discover how to open spaces for persons in the plurality, spaces where they can become different, where they can grow. (p. 56)

The "spaces" that Greene celebrates serves as our referent for an authentic, nurturing culture. Just as there are over 120 definitions of curriculum in the curriculum studies literature, there is a diverse set of definitions of culture in the cultural studies literature. We are working with a cultural interpretation that fits our fourfold process. In her study of "cultures of curriculum," Joseph (2000b) writes:

There are rarely "pure" cultures that develop without influences from others, people may be unaware of how they learn their culture, and they may find it hard to discern patterns of beliefs and behaviors that seem normal to them. More importantly, although people may share similar understandings of their societies and everyday life and hold shared values, individuals construe their own personal interpretations of events, practices, and symbols; they are not merely docile actors in a scripted cultural play but dynamic creators of meaning. Thus, when thinking about a school or classroom, we must simultaneously imagine not a static entity but an assemblage of individuals who have different family cultures, different understandings and values influenced by race or ethnicity, gender, class, and religion as well as their own creativity and imagination. (p. 18)

The educational culture—perhaps more accurately described as subculture—that we have in mind nurtures this active meaning making. Such a culture is defined by dynamic, growth-oriented social interactions grounded in democratic values. It may not be possible to formally organize such a supportive culture in an educational institution. If so, the organizing work may need to be practiced informally by a small group of educators, perhaps in collaboration with other curriculum stakeholders such as students' parents. At a minimum, such informal organizing could be the creation of an informal study-and-practice partnership between two colleagues.

Joseph (2000b) cites Spindler and Spindler's (1987) definition of culture as "a continuing dialogue that revolves around pivotal areas of concern in a given community" (p. 17). This is an important interpretation of culture in our theoretical platform due to the adult developmental nature of the fourfold process. Our research has documented the fact that the critical shift from a standardized management orientation often involves a pivot to subject-centered orientations—generally called "constructivist best practices" (Wiggins & McTighe, 2005)—before there is a final embrace of 3S pedagogical artistry (Henderson & Gornik, 2007). Educators may need to first gain experience with teaching for subject understandings before they are ready to think about teaching for subject understandings that are deepened by democratic self and social understandings.

Kuhn's (1962) concept of "paradigm shift" provides insight into these three pivots. Kuhn documents the way that scientific communities are guided by a "puzzle-solving" framework that is guided by a dominant "exemplar." The exemplar has two functions: it posits the organizing problem for a particular disciplinary culture, and it presents a way to study and, perhaps, solve the puzzle. Kuhn's thesis is that a particular scientific culture advances in a "paradigm shifting" way that can be unpredictable, tension-filled, and highly politicized. Brown (1988) insightfully summarizes Kuhn's thesis:

Only in crisis does the scientific community abandon its normal, puzzle-solving rules. Some members . . . inaugurate a deliberate scrutiny of fundamental assumptions. . . . An innovator may come forward with a revolutionary new paradigm. . . . The crisis moves to resolution as certain community members switch loyalties to the new paradigm. Once adhering to the new paradigm, these community members are in a "new world," incommensurable with the old one. At first slowly, they eventually attend to increasingly divergent problems, apply novel methods, and think in new terms. (p. 19)

Our fourfold process involves a paradigm shift from standardized management to practical wisdom with, perhaps, a commitment to constructivist best practices as an intermediary step. This shouldn't be surprising since a concern for a broad, holistic democratic education would definitely challenge the undemocratic socio-emotional dimensions in curricular contexts. Undemocratic "habituated values" (Ryan, 2011, p. 65) may pervade these contexts but remain hidden from view or unacknowledged. These two educational possibilities are called hidden and null curricula in curriculum studies. Joseph (2000a) provides several illustrations:

The *implicit* [hidden] curriculum is the learning and interaction that occurs that is not explicitly announced in school programs. Implicit curriculum may be intentionally taught—for example, a teacher, fearful of confrontation from the very conservative community in which she works, continually tries to teach critical thinking but never announces these goals to parents or students. Implicit curriculum may also be inadvertent, such as when teachers may not realize how classrooms or schools teach competition as a social value. The *null* curriculum deals with what is systematically excluded, neglected, or not considered. Thus, teachers create a null curriculum when they teach history as "the true story" but do not present the perspectives of peoples from non-dominant cultures—or choose as "the greatest literature" only works written by European males. (p. 4)

The paradigm-shifting nature of our definition of an authentic culture that nurtures 3S pedagogy clarifies an important critical distinction in our theoretical platform. The fourfold process is an interpretation of curriculum leadership, not instructional leadership (Henderson, 2010). Our pivotal area of concern is with a holistic education that extends beyond subject learning into self and social learning. Instructional leadership, which is the paradigmatic orientation in current leadership studies literature, is not sufficiently broad for our purposes. Ylimaki's (2011) comprehensive definition of "critical curriculum leadership" informs the fourfold process:

Curriculum leadership involves three interrelated dimensions: curriculum theory, the role of politics, and leadership identity, all of which are informed by socio-cultural and political influences . . . particular community contexts, and school cultures. (p. 19)

Just as there are multiple definitions of curriculum and culture in the curriculum and cultural studies literature, there are many interpretations of leadership in the leadership studies literature. We believe Donaldson's (2001) definition of educational leadership is particularly useful in explaining and justifying the fourfold process. Donaldson sets the stage for his leadership interpretation with a critique of standardized management in education, which he calls the "bureaucratic paradigm." He challenges four "tenets" of this paradigm:

> Leadership is invested in individuals occupying formally appointed roles. . . . Leaders have greater knowledge and can make better judgments than those they lead. . . . Leaders manage a rationally organized system for production that will maximize outputs by running with maximum efficiency. . . . Leaders optimize the production of student results by this system through a command-and-control pyramid structure. (p. 33)

Donaldson concludes his critique of these four tenets with this assertion: "American public schools are unusual types of organization. They function more on moral conviction and professional judgment than they do on tightly prescribed goals and technical rationality" (p. 39). Our notion of authentic cultures that nurture 3S pedagogical artistry is based on this organizational insight.

Following his critique of the bureaucratic paradigm, Donaldson introduces an interpretation of educational leadership, which he metaphorically describes as the confluence of "streams" creating a strong river:

> The relational stream carries emotional and interpersonal connections toward . . . collective effort. The purposive stream bears peoples' intellectual and philosophical predilections. . . . This stream flows with ideals and aspirations, so I see it playing above and even beyond the reach of the relational stream. It engages members in learning, planning, and acting for improvement, supported by strong relationships and a robust purpose. So I visualize it at the center of the leadership river, flowing forward on the strength of relationships towards goals inspired by purpose. Leaders' work lies in the interweaving of these streams into one strong current. (p. 53)

This "strong river" is the image we have of the generative lead-learning in our fourfold process. As vividly portrayed in Donaldson's book, it is an image of teachers and administrators working with one another and with other curriculum stakeholders on an inspiring educational purpose: *the nurturance of a teaching artistry that fosters students' emerging vocational artistries.*

The leadership studies scholar, Catherine Hackney, begins her essay on generative leadership with this quote from Klimek, Ritzenhein, and Sullivan's (2008) book:

> Generative leadership becomes a way of being rather than just a new set of techniques for doing the work of a leader. . . . Generative school leaders are intent on actualizing the generative capacity of their school for one simple reason: they realize that both students and staff will learn, perform, and thrive better. Generative environments are rich in stimuli, offering challenges and contrasts to existing mental models that can catalyze new ideas and new avenues for action. Generative leaders push back on the commonplace mechanistic ways of organizing and doing business to make room for generative modes of inquiry and action. (pp. 15, 48)

After discussing and critically analyzing a rich career of generative leadership as a middle school teacher, elementary school principal, and associate dean in a college of education, Hackney (2015) concludes her essay with this strong professional assertion:

> We must practice *connected knowing* (Belenky, Clinchy, Goldberger, & Tarule, 1986) that cultivates an environment of reciprocity, humility, and generosity toward others. We, as teachers and principals, must muster up the courage to promote and "protect our good work" (Schwartz & Sharpe, 2010, p. 287), for our profession, but most especially, for all of the students we serve. Taking the long view, we educators must become generative, democratic leaders for our organizations and for our societies. (p. 174)

In the context of this book's fourfold process, this generative leadership is interpreted as a "connected" lead-learning that is focused on building capacities for 3S pedagogical excellence. Simply stated, 3S pedagogy requires disciplined study and practice. There may be a few teachers who are "born" to practice this professional artistry, but this would be quite rare. Most teachers, and we include the three of us co-writing this book, must work hard over many years to achieve this professional excellence; and when it comes to 3S pedagogical artistry, there's always more developmental work that can be done.

It took 27 years of teaching experience to get to the point of being able to compose this theoretical platform; and as Eisner (2005) points out in one of his last published essays, this should not be surprising:

> Phronesis, the development of wise practical reasoning, is better suited to what teachers do and need. . . . [Such] artistry is most likely when we acknowledge its relevance to teaching and create the conditions in schools in which teachers can learn to think like artists. . . . The long-term heart of teacher education is

not primarily the university; it is the workplace, the school, the place in which teachers spend the better part of their lives. . . . The creation of schools in which the growth of teachers is taken seriously will require evolution: it will take time to learn how to create them. To create such places a new kind of school culture will have to be crafted, a culture that cares as much about the growth of teachers as the growth of students. I mentioned the word culture. You know what a culture is. A culture in the biological sense is a medium for growing things. A culture in the anthropological sense is a shared way of life. Schools need to create a shared way of life that provides a medium for growing teachers, for ultimately the growth of students will go no farther than the growth of those who teach them. (p. 203)

Our research over the years has identified a capacity-building agenda that is particularly important for the growth of 3S pedagogical artistry: the cultivation of specific conceptual, reflective, and virtuous repertoires. Though we acknowledge that other developmental topics could be relevant, our focus is on this three-part professional growth. This capacity building is a particular application of a new policy paradigm known as the "capabilities approach," which is being advanced by Martha Nussbaum and her "human development" associates. Nussbaum (2011) describes this approach as a "social justice" orientation that, "takes *each person as an end*, asking not just about the total or average well-being but about the opportunities available to each person. It is *focused on choice or freedom*, holding that the crucial good societies should be promoting for their people is a set of opportunities, or substantial freedoms, which people then may or may not exercise in action: the choice is theirs" (p. 18).

We believe in treating teachers and their supportive curriculum stakeholders, particularly educational administrators, as valuable human development resources. From the perspective of creating an authentic culture that nurtures the capacity building that 3S pedagogical excellence requires, we want all stakeholders to have the growth opportunities that they need.

Such a platform statement is obvious for teachers' and students' journeys of understanding, but it may not be as apparent for administrators' development. However, our research clearly demonstrates that the cultivation of educational administrators' conceptual, reflective, and virtuous repertoires is equally important (Gornik & Samford, in press). As noted by Donaldson (2001) in his critique of the "bureaucratic paradigm," administrators are key gatekeepers in the current standardized management cultures. Therefore, if teachers are going to have organizational support to study and practice 3S pedagogy, they will need their administrators' approval and proactive backing; but to repeat an earlier point, if official administrative support is not forthcoming, teachers can still seek out small-scale, informal developmental opportunities.

With reference to this book's introductory and theoretical platform chapters, the question of what constitutes the necessary conceptual repertoire is easily explained. It is all the concepts that have been introduced in these two chapters. Our research has clearly documented the cognitive dissonance that teachers and administrators can experience as they are being introduced to 3S pedagogy and its central conceptual location in the practical wisdom paradigm. Paradigm shifts are not easy because, in part, they require learning new concepts. In the early part of the twentieth century, there were physicists who had acquired their expertise in the context of the Newtonian paradigm and who experienced so much dissonance with Einstein's theorizing that they committed suicide. Educators who are comfortable with such management concepts as curriculum mapping, testing achievement, and teacher accountability may find it difficult at first to understand the critically informed concepts in this text's first two chapters. With reference to the third fold, the big developmental question is: *who is willing to undertake the necessary journey of understanding?*

Through years of action research, we have created and refined a reflective repertoire that is an essential feature of 3S pedagogical artistry. This repertoire, which involves three forms of reflective inquiry informed by four deliberative conversations, is an integration of the work of John Dewey, Joseph Schwab, and William Pinar (Henderson et al., 2015). There is a section in Dewey's *How We Think* titled "Reflective Thinking Impels to Inquiry." In this section, Dewey (1933) argues that reflection deepened through inquiry is a key feature of good problem solving. He illustrates his point by referring to Christopher Columbus' persistent questioning of the pervasive belief that the world was flat:

> The . . . belief in the flatness of the earth had some foundation in evidence; it rested upon what men could see easily within the limits of their vision. But this evidence was not further looked into; it was not checked by considering other evidence; there was no search for new evidence. Ultimately, the [flatness] belief rested on laziness, inertia, custom, absence of courage, and energy in investigation. (p. 8)

Dewey concludes his analysis of this synergy between reflection and inquiry with this comprehensive definition of reflective thinking: "*Active, persistent, and careful consideration of any belief or supposed form of knowledge in the light of the grounds that support it and the further conclusions to which it tends*" (p. 9).

Reflective inquiry is a concept that educators can quickly understand (Henderson, 2001); and as we began working with the notion of 3S pedagogy, our research clearly indicated the relevance of three key areas of professional reflection: reflective inquiry on how to *teach* for 3S understandings, on how to *model* such holistic journeys of understanding for one's students, and on how to *communicate* the power of this pedagogical artistry to colleagues and other curriculum stakeholders. Consequently, we created lead-learning guidance on how to engage in this reflective teaching, modeling, and communicating (Henderson et al., 2015), and this work will be featured in our montage guidance.

Our lengthy action research on the three reflective inquiries clarified the importance of incorporating four deliberative conversations into this three-part reflective inquiry; and as we briefly noted earlier, our use of the "deliberative conversation" concept is a synthesis of Schwab's work on deliberative artistry and Pinar's work on curriculum as conversations. Our research documents the importance of engaging in four deliberative conversations as key features 3S pedagogical reflections: how to *negotiate the paradigmatic tensions* between management and wisdom problem solving, how to incorporate *social justice* into teaching-learning transactions, how to practice a *democratic humanism* that rejects all forms of a degrading "othering," and how to become better attuned to the *caring aesthetics* embedded in 3S pedagogical relations. We created lead-learning guidance on how to practice these four important considerations (Henderson et al., 2015), and this work is incorporated into our montage advice and recommendations.

Work on the virtuous repertoire in our montage guidance began in 1997. Six curriculum scholars collaborated with eight Vermont curriculum leaders on the topic of democratic curriculum leadership (Henderson & Kesson, 1999). A key finding of this project was the importance of wise practical judgments in education, and this topic was subsequently clarified and narratively illustrated in Henderson and Kesson's (2004) *Curriculum Wisdom: Educational Decisions in Democratic Societies*. Eleven years later, in 2015, an international team of eighteen educators collaborated on a book that addressed the reconceptualization of curriculum development from the perspective of democratic practical wisdom. This work was summarized as follows:

> Practical wisdom as a general normative referent for all human actions has an ancient pedigree, tracing back to Aristotle's *Nicomachean Ethics*, which was published around 340 BCE. Arguing that the exercise of practical wisdom is critical for staying centered on the balanced, "golden mean" of the virtuous life and for the happiness and flourishing that results from this way of being, Aristotle (2011) writes: "He who is a good deliberator simply is skilled in aiming, in accord with calculation, at what is best for a human being in things attainable through action." (Henderson et al. 2015, pp. 17–18)

It's Aristotle's ethical insight that the pursuit of practical wisdom involves a set of virtues. Current research on 3S pedagogy, which is being conducted through a three-year teacher leadership grant funded by the Ohio Department of Education (2015–2018), has identified Roberts and Wood's (2007) analysis of seven Aristotelian virtues as a key referent for the development of 3S pedagogical artistry. The seven virtues are: love of knowledge, firmness, courage and caution, humility, autonomy, generosity, and practical wisdom.

The love of knowledge refers to the embrace of disciplined study and knowing; while firmness refers to the eclectic, deliberative adjustment of habits and customs in light of new knowledge. Courage and caution are necessary to advance new knowledge by thoughtfully balancing traditional and progressive perspectives. The virtue of humility is, "a disposition not to make unwarranted intellectual entitlement claims on the basis of one's (supposed) superiority or excellence" (Roberts & Wood, 2007, p. 250). Autonomy is displayed "by the student or researcher who is able to work on his [her] own . . . [embracing] the intelligence and knowledge of others as needed; but it also means an intelligent ability to stand one's own ground against bullying, as well as gentler forms of pressure to conform" (p. 258).

Generosity is the ability "to give valuable things—material goods, time, attention, energy, concessions, credit, the benefit of a doubt, knowledge—to other persons" (p. 286); and the culminating virtue, practical wisdom "is involved in every virtue, as constituting the good judgment without which no human virtue could be exemplified in action, emotion, or judgment" (p. 305). In sum, practical wisdom "is a disposition to adjudicate well, in the concrete circumstances of life, between the concerns characteristic of intellectual practices and more broadly human concerns" (p. 312). Our montage guidance will provide practical illustrations and advice on the cultivation of these seven virtues.

Fourth Fold: Participatory Evaluating

The presentation of our theoretical platform culminates with an explanation of the fourth fold in the problem-solving process, which we are calling "participatory evaluating" and which is organized around the following question: how are we democratically reviewing the diversified expressive outcomes and impacts of this pedagogical artistry? Schwandt (2015) argues that comprehensive evaluation focuses on both outcomes and impacts:

> *Outcomes* are changes that occur directly as a result of inputs, activities, and outputs, such as expected changes in attitudes, behaviors, knowledge, skills, status, or level of functioning. . . . Often outcomes are further divided into im-

mediate and intermediate—the form usually referring to changes in attitudes, skills, knowledge, and the latter referring to actual behavioral changes that will lead to long-term *impacts*. (p. 37)

We agree with this broad approach to educational evaluation; and given our problem-solving focus on professional awakening, holistic pedagogy, and capacity building, we are working with particular interpretations of outcomes and impacts. Because our interest is in educators' and students' journeys of 3S understanding, Eisner's (1994b) distinction between behavioral objectives and expressive outcomes is quite relevant. Setting the stage for his definition of expressive outcomes, Eisner begins by offering a thoughtful critique of Robert Mager's argument for the use of precise behavioral objectives in education. Mager (1962) writes that, "The statement of objectives of a training program must denote *measurable* attributes *observable* in the graduates of the program" (p. 31). Eisner (1994b) responds with this balanced perspective: "When specific skills or competencies are appropriate, such [behavioral] objectives can be formulated, but one should not feel compelled to abandon educational aims that cannot be reduced to measureable forms of predictable performance" (p. 113).

Eisner's critical point is that educators should not feel forced to work with precise behavioral objectives when their deliberations indicate more relevant and productive evaluative alternatives. Such professional judgments are guided by making a distinction between training and education. There are times when students may need specific training interventions. For example, teaching to standardized tests may be warranted on certain occasions in certain contexts. However, teaching for 3S understanding involves a personal and transactional "leading out of" and "leading into" that touches on the etymological source of the pedagogical term. Max van Manen (1991) explains:

The original Greek idea of pedagogy has associated with it the meaning of *leading* in the sense of accompanying the child and living with the child in such a way as to provide direction and care for his or her life. . . . [The child] must eventually grow out of (*educere*: to lead out of) the world of childhood. My world of adulthood becomes an invitation, a beckoning to the child (*educare*: to lead into). Leading means going first, and in going first you can trust me, for I have tested the ice.

Returning to Eisner's (1994b) argument concerning meaningful evaluative deliberations on educational objectives, he writes:

Outcomes are essentially what one ends up with, intended or not, after some form of engagement. Expressive outcomes are the consequences of curriculum activities that are intentionally planned to provide a fertile field for personal purposing and experience. . . . Expressive activities precede rather than follow expressive outcomes. The tack taken with respect to the generation of expressive outcomes is to create activities that are sufficiently rich to allow for a wide, productive range of educationally valuable outcomes. (pp. 118–20)

We work with an "expressive outcome" framework in our montage guidance, particularly with reference to teachers' and students' expressions of their journeys of 3S understanding.

We recognize that such expressions may naturally take a narrative form. However, other "forms of representation" (Eisner, 1994a) may also be relevant. Eisner defines this concept and explains its importance in educational equity:

> What we ought to develop, in my view, is the student's ability to access meaning within the variety of forms of representation that humans use to represent the contents of their consciousness. These forms are no less important in the fine arts than they are in the sciences; they are no less important in mathematics than they are in the humanities. Further, the provision of opportunities to learn how to use such literacies ought to contribute to greater educational equity for students, especially for those whose aptitudes reside in the use of forms of representation now marginalized by our current educational priorities. (p. x)

We will be working with this broad liberal arts, pluralistic interpretation of literacy as we offer guidance on how to evaluate 3S pedagogical *outcomes*.

As we have already noted, the fourfold process is a recursive circuit of valuation based on Dewey's view of democracy as not just a form of government but a moral way of living. Consequently, there is an overarching value-based question concerning the quality of the fourfold problem solving: *what long-term personal, interpersonal, institutional, community, and societal impacts are we educators making through our awakening, teaching, and capacity-building efforts?* This question will guide the montage guidance we have created for this fourth fold in the process.

We are using the term "reviewing" in our organizing question to make the point that the evaluation of 3S pedagogy involves a continuous, holistic monitoring. Stake's (2004) argument for an evaluation approach that is "responsive" to the complexities of *what* one is evaluating informs this important principle: "The task for the evaluator is not to have the last word, but to describe effectively and usefully the diverse aspects of quality in the program" (p. 178). Schwandt (2015) summarizes Stake's interpretation of responsive evaluation as follows: "It is therefore the task of the evaluator to capture those ways of perceiving quality and to offer a holistic portrayal of this complex understanding of overall value in such a way that it is accessible to the immediate stakeholders in a program" (p. 61). Schwandt goes on to note that working in this holistic way involves deliberative judgments that are grounded in an "all-things-considered" eclecticism: "To state it formally, a program (*X*) is considered valuable when every way in which *X* could be valuable is weighed one against the other" (p. 61). This holistic, deliberative eclecticism is nurtured through a broad and diverse democratic participation. This is why we are advancing a highly participatory approach to educational evaluation.

The participatory evaluation we have in mind involves administrators and teachers working closely with one another, with students, and with all other relevant curriculum stakeholders. As Schwandt (2015) notes, this is a highly democratic approach:

> Deliberative approaches are one means of reaching an all-things-considered judgment. Deliberation broadly defined as a process for achieving democracy . . . [means] that the views of program beneficiaries are included in delibera-tions . . . [since] evaluation ought to serve social justice. This is a prescriptive approach to valuing. (pp. 61–62)

Democratic educational evaluation is informed by House and Howe's (2000) critical point that, "the more extensive the deliberation is, the better would be the findings we expect to emerge. For the most part, there is not enough deliberation in evaluation rather than too much" (p. 11). House and Howe's deliberative insight raises an important issue on the importance of highly participatory deliberations when evaluating the outcomes and im-pacts of 3S pedagogy.

Eisner's (1994b) advocacy for "educational criticism" informed by "edu-cational connoisseurship" also provides a powerful, public way to practice participatory evaluations of 3S pedagogy. Eisner argues that the heritage of art criticism can be applied to educational evaluation:

> Educational criticism . . . [is a] form of educational inquiry, a species of educa-tional evaluation . . . [that] is qualitative in character . . . and takes its lead from the work that critics have done in literature, theater, film, music, and the visual arts. (p. 212)

On the connoisseurship side of this evaluative coin, the evaluator creates a refined qualitative language "that will help others perceive the work more deeply" (Eisner, 1994b, p. 213). For example, a connoisseur of 3S pedagogy might pursue the following question: what are the subtle qualities of students' subject understandings deepened by democratic self and social understand-ings? On the critical side of this evaluative coin, Eisner notes that the goal is "the illumination of something's qualities so that an appraisal of its value can be made" (p. 214). With reference to 3S pedagogy, a follow-up to the above question might be: what are the long-term values of the students' holistic understandings, and are there emergent vocational artistries that these understandings foreshadow?

Eisner (1994b) makes a concluding point about the practice of educational connoisseurship and criticism that is quite important for the fourfold process: "As one ceases using stock responses to educational situations and develops habits of perceptual exploration, the ability to experience qualities and their relationships increases" (p. 242). The participatory evaluating we have in mind goes far beyond "stock responses" of standardized test evaluations. Our term, participatory evaluating, refers to the practice of deliberative judgments that are based on a rigorous "perceptual exploration" of subject understandings deepened by democratic self and social understandings. We imagine future public schools celebrating students' performances of 3S understandings the way current American public schools celebrate boys' football and basketball championships.

Such evaluative work is not only important for teachers, students, and administrators but for all curriculum stakeholders, including the general public. All members of a democratically oriented society need to think deeply about the long-term values of education. Stated another way, all citizens should have educational experiences with circuits of democratic valuation; all citizens must be educated for a democratic way of life through purposeful, experiential learning. Consequently, there is a key evaluative question for societies with democratic aspirations: *are students in particular educational programs authentically experiencing a democratic way of life in their daily informal and formal learning activities?*

Elliot Eisner's *The Educational Imagination: On the Design and Evaluation of School Programs* was first published in 1979. He refined his understanding of educational connoisseurship and criticism in a 1991 publication titled *The Enlightened Eye: Qualitative Inquiry and the Enhancement of Educational Practice*. This latter book was reprinted in 2017 with a Foreword by Nel Noddings. Noddings (2017) celebrates the public, democratic value of Eisner's educational connoisseurship and criticism:

> *The Enlightened Eye* aims to open our eyes, pique our imagination, and encourage critical thought. With enhanced perception, reflection, and imagination, researchers and practitioners are better positioned to work collaboratively toward richer forms of education. [Eisner's] educational criticism is especially important in the current climate of schooling in which teachers are ordered to use a specific learning objective for every lesson, test constantly, record test results, and retest. Are the students bored? Are teachers frustrated? Are there

better practices available? Eisner concludes this book with words pertinent to today's educational problems: "By broadening the forms through which the educational world is described, interpreted, and appraised, and by diversifying the methods through which content is made available and teaching methods are used, the politics of practice become more generous" (p. 246). We can hope that the educational community listens. (p. ix)

This hope for the educational community, and for all members of democratically aspiring societies, underlies our guidance for the participatory evaluation in the fourfold process.

SUMMARY STATEMENT

We conclude our presentation of the theoretical platform that frames our montage guidance with a brief summary statement on the fourfold process. Our summary is inspired by this excerpt from John Dewey's last published essay:

There is a great deal of talk about education being a cooperative enterprise in which teachers and students participate democratically, but there is far more talk about it than the doing of it. . . . To change long-established habits in the individual is a slow, difficult and complicated process. To change long-established institutions—which are social habits organized in the structure of the common life—is a much slower, more difficult and far more complicated process. . . . For the creation of a democratic society we need an educational system where the process of moral-intellectual development is in practice as in theory a cooperative transaction of inquiry engaged in by free, independent human beings who treat ideas and the heritage of the past as means and methods for the further enrichment of life, quantitatively and qualitatively, who use the good attained for the discovery and establishment of something better. (1952, pp. viii–xi)

Nearing the end of his life, Dewey critiques empty progressive rhetoric, recognizes the deep challenges of personal and social change, and envisions "a cooperative transaction of inquiry" in education that nurtures and enriches holistic, democratic living. Dewey's critical pragmatism has stood the test of time, and our fourfold process is a particular way of enacting his vision of transactional artistry. Time will tell as to whether or not our interpretation, which is based on an integration of curriculum, teaching, and leadership perspectives, has any enduring value.

We have now provided an extensive, and perhaps at times daunting, conceptual explanation of the fourfold process. To provide a snapshot of this theoretical big picture, we offer the following summary of the key features of each fold. The first fold in our problem-solving process invites and encourages an awakening to education as a pivotal professional art in societies with democratic aspirations. The focus is on critical consciousness-raising that challenges the compliant semi-professionalism fostered by standardized accountability systems. This fold invites complicated, clarifying conversations on the holistic purposes of democratic education.

The second fold invites and encourages the holistic teaching that this deep purposing summons. The focus is on the pursuit of a pedagogical artistry that is grounded in creative transactional relations between teachers and students. Teachers gain experience with 3S pedagogy by providing students with experiences that facilitate their Subject understandings deepened by democratic Self and Social understandings. When students cultivate their 3S understandings, they enter powerful educational pathways for discovering and refining their vocational callings. In short, 3S pedagogy is a vocational artistry that fosters students' vocational artistries.

The third fold invites and encourages the capacity building that the practice of 3S pedagogical artistry requires. This developmental focus is on the cultivation of essential conceptual, reflective, and virtuous repertoires through a study-and-practice agenda advanced by lead-learning initiatives and support. This generative leadership is organized around nurturing the emergence of democratic practical wisdom.

The fourth fold invites and encourages an eclectic, deliberative evaluation of the expressive outcomes and long-term impacts of the journeys of understanding that are the heart and soul of the problem-solving process, and we will have more to say about the value of this personal journeying both in the following montage chapters and in our book's epilogue. A key purpose of this highly participatory evaluative work is the humanistic enlightenment of *all* curriculum stakeholders.

REFERENCES

Aristotle. (2011). *Aristotle's Nicomachean ethics.* (R. C. Bartlett & S. D. Collins, Trans.). Chicago, IL: University of Chicago Press.

Belenky, M. F., Clinchy, B. M., Goldberger, N. R., & Tarule, J. M. (1986). *Women's ways of knowing: The development of self, voice, and mind.* New York, NY: Basic Books.

Brown, T. M. (1988). How fields change: A critique of the "Kuhnian" view. In W. F. Pinar (Ed.), *Contemporary curriculum discourses* (pp. 16–30). Scottsdale, AZ: Gorsuch Scarisbrick.

Colby, A., & Sullivan, W. M. (2008). Formation of professionalism and purpose perspective from the Preparation for the Professions Program. *University of St. Thomas Law Journal, 5,* 404–27.

Dewey, J. (1933). *How we think: A restatement of the relation of reflective thinking to the educative process.* Boston, MA: D.C. Heath & Company. (Original work published 1910)

————. (1938). *Logic: The theory of inquiry.* New York, NY: Henry Holt & Company.

————. (1943). *The school and society* (rev. ed.). Chicago, IL: University of Chicago Press.

————. (1952). Introduction. In E. R. Clapp, *The use of resources in education* (pp. vii–xi). New York, NY: Harper & Brothers.

————. (1958). *Art as experience.* New York, NY: Capricorn Books. (Original work published 1935)

————. (1966). Appendix II: The theory of the Chicago experiment. In K. C. Mayhew & A. C. Edwards, *The Dewey school: The laboratory school of the University of Chicago, 1896–1903* (pp. 463–77). New York, NY: Atherton Press. (Original work published 1936)

Donaldson, G. A., Jr. (2008). *Cultivating leadership in schools: Connecting people, purpose, and practice.* New York, NY: Teachers College Press.

Eisner, E. W. (1994a). *Cognition and curriculum reconsidered* (2nd ed.). New York, NY: Teachers College Press.

————. (1994b). *The educational imagination: On the design and evaluation of school programs* (3rd ed.). New York, NY: Macmillan.

————. (2005). *Reimagining schools: The selected works of Elliot Eisner.* New York, NY: Routledge.

Gadamer, H. G. (1975). *Truth and method.* (G. Barden & J. Cumming, Eds. & Trans.). New York, NY: Seabury.

Goodwin, D. K. (2005). *Team of rivals: The political genius of Abraham Lincoln.* New York, NY: Simon & Schuster.

Gornik, R., & Samford, W. (In press). *Into the light: Creating a culture of support for teacher leaders.* Lanham, MD: Rowman & Littlefield.

Greene, M. (1988). *The dialectic of freedom.* New York, NY: Teachers College Press.

————. (2017). Curriculum and consciousness. In D. J. Flinders & S. J. Thornton (Eds.), *The curriculum studies reader* (5th ed., pp. 147–59). New York, NY: Routledge. (Original work published 1971)

Hackney, C. E. (2015). Generative leadership: Protecting the good work. In J. G. Henderson et al., *Reconceptualizing curriculum development: Inspiring and informing action* (pp. 169–74). New York, NY: Routledge.

Henderson, J. G. (2001). *Reflective teaching: Professional artistry through inquiry.* Columbus, OH: Merrill/Prentice Hall.

Henderson, J. G. (2010). Curriculum leadership. In G. Kridel (Ed.), *Encyclopedia of curriculum studies* (Vol. 1, pp. 220–24). Los Angeles, CA: Sage.

Henderson, J. G., & Gornik, R. (2007). *Transformative curriculum leadership* (3rd ed.). Upper Saddle River, NJ: Merrill/Prentice Hall.

Henderson, J. G., & Kesson, K. R. (Eds.). (1999). *Understanding democratic curriculum leadership.* New York, NY: Teachers College Press.

Henderson, J. G., & Kesson, K. R. (2004). *Curriculum wisdom: Educational decisions in democratic societies.* Upper Saddle River, NJ: Merrill/Prentice Hall.

Henderson, J. G., et al. (2015). *Reconceptualizing curriculum development: Inspiring and informing action.* New York, NY: Routledge.

House, E. R., & Howe, K. R. (2000). Deliberative democratic evaluation. In K. E. Ryan & L. DeStefano (Eds.), *Evaluation as a democratic process: Promoting inclusion, dialogue, and deliberation* (pp. 3–12). San Francisco, CA: Jossey-Bass.

Joseph, P. B. (2000a). Conceptualizing curriculum. In P. B. Joseph, S. L. Bravmann, M. A. Windschitl, E. A. Mikel, & N. S. Green, *Cultures of curriculum* (pp. 1–14). Mahwah, NJ: Lawrence Erlbaum Associates.

———. (2000b). Understanding curriculum as culture. In P. B. Joseph, S. L. Bravmann, M. A. Windschitl, E. A. Mikel, & N. S. Green, *Cultures of curriculum* (pp. 15–27). Mahwah, NJ: Lawrence Erlbaum Associates.

Kirylo, J. D. (2016). *Teaching with purpose: An inquiry into the who, why, and how we teach.* Lanham, MD: Rowman & Littlefield.

Klimek, K. J., Ritzenhein, E., & Sullivan, K. D. (2008). *Generative leadership: Shaping new futures for today's schools.* Thousand Oaks, CA: Corwin Press.

Kuhn, T. S. (1962). *The structure of scientific revolutions.* Chicago, IL: University of Chicago Press.

Lortie, D. C. (1975). *Schoolteachers: A sociological study.* Chicago, IL: University of Chicago Press.

Mager, R. (1962). *Preparing instructional objectives.* Palo Alto, CA: Fearon.

McClintock, R. (1971). Toward a place for study in a world of instruction. *Teachers College Record, 73*(2), 161–205.

Morris, M. (2016). *Curriculum studies guidebooks, Volume 1: Concepts and theoretical frameworks.* New York, NY: Peter Lang.

Nancy, J. (2000). *Being singular plural.* (R. D. Richardson & A. E. O'Byrne, Trans.). Stanford, CA: Stanford University Press.

Noddings, N. (2013). *Education and democracy in the 21st century.* New York, NY: Teachers College Press.

Noddings, N. (2017). Foreword. In E. W. Eisner, *The enlightened eye: Qualitative inquiry and the enhancement of educational practice* (p. ix). New York, NY: Teachers College Press.

Nussbaum, M. C. (2011). *Creating capabilities: The human development approach.* Cambridge, MA: Belknap Press.

Paraskeva, J. M. (2016). *Curriculum epistemicide: Towards an itinerant curriculum theory.* New York, NY: Routledge.

Pinar, W. F. (Ed.). (2000). *Curriculum studies: The reconceptualization.* Troy, NY: Educator's International Press.

———. (2006). *The synoptic text today and other essays: Curriculum development after the reconceptualization.* New York, NY: Peter Lang.

Pinar, W. F., Reynolds, W. M., Slattery, P., & Taubman, P. M. (1995). *Understanding curriculum: An introduction to the study of historical and contemporary curriculum discourses.* New York, NY: Peter Lang.

Pink, D. H. (2009). *Drive: The surprising truth about what motivates us*. New York, NY: Penguin Group.

Rancière, J. (2010). *Dissensus: On politics and aesthetics*. (S. Corcoran, Ed. & Trans.). London, England: Continuum.

Roberts, R. C., & Wood, W. J. (2007). *Intellectual virtues: An essay in regulative epistemology*. New York, NY: Clarendon Press.

Ryan, F. X. (2011). *Seeing together: Mind, matter and the experimental outlook of John Dewey and Arthur F. Bentley*. Great Barrington, MA: American Institute for Economic Research.

Schubert, W. H. (1986). *Curriculum: Perspective, paradigm, and possibility*. New York, NY: Macmillan.

Schwab, J. J. (1978). *Science, curriculum, and liberal education*. Chicago, IL: University of Chicago Press.

Schwandt, T. A. (2015). *Evaluation foundations revisited: Cultivating a life of the mind for practice*. Stanford, CA: Stanford University Press.

Schwartz, B., & Sharpe, K. (2010). *Practical wisdom: The right way to do the right thing*. New York, NY: Riverhead Books.

Spindler, G., & Spindler, L. (1987). Ethnography: An anthropological view. In G. D. Spindler (Ed.), *Education and cultural process: Anthropological approaches* (2nd ed., pp. 151–56). Prospect Heights, IL: Waveland.

Stake, R. E. (2004). *Standards-based and responsive evaluation*. Newbury Park, CA: Sage.

van Manen, M. (1991). *The tact of teaching: The meaning of pedagogical thoughtfulness*. Albany, NY: State University of New York Press.

Walker, D. F. (1971, November). The process of curriculum development: A naturalistic model. *School Review, 80*, 51–65.

Walker, D. F., & Soltis, J. F. (2009). *Curriculum and aims* (5th ed.). New York, NY: Teachers College Press.

Wiggins, G., & McTighe, J. (2005). *Understanding by design* (2nd ed.). Alexandria, VA: Association for Supervision and Curriculum Development.

Ylimaki, R. M. (2011). *Critical curriculum leadership: A framework for progressive education*. New York, NY: Routledge.

Chapter Two

Professional Awakening

How are we awakening to a professionally compelling, holistic interpretation of educational purpose?

Each one of us enters the field of education for various reasons. Some of us go into education because we have a desire to make a difference in the world. Others of us had inspirational teachers growing up, and we wanted to become educators because of them. For some the opposite may be true—becoming educators because we want to be better than the ones we had. Some of us have a deep passion for a particular subject area and want to share that with future generations. Still yet, others of us may go into the profession for a stable career. Some go directly into schools upon finishing a degree and stay at the same school for an entire career. Others of us transition to different schools, different positions in schools, or perhaps end up in different regions or countries. Some of us may even come to education after a career change or two.

We, as authors, readily recognize that readers are on different paths and are not blank slates with regards to their educational experiences, understandings, expectations, and dreams. You, along with every student, teacher, and administrator is a node in the discipline of education who possess a unique vantage point that beckons for deliberation and serious consideration. The professional awakening fold offers us an opportunity to meditate on our viewpoints—a space where our memories from the past and perceptions of the present meet an ever-emerging future. Professional awakening, simultaneously, calls us to critically engage with the educational practices we engage in and see happening around us. This fold, in short, is about awakening ourselves to holistic, democratic interpretations of educational purposes while enlivening our understandings with a sense of professional agency.

WHAT'S IN OUR EDUCATIONAL PURPOSES?

To begin with, let us take a step back for a moment and consider a flurry of questions about education. What are the driving purposes of education? Why do these exists? Who cares about them? Who decided on these educational purposes? Why do purposes matter at all? Even more basic yet, what is education anyway? Is it a science, an art, or maybe both? Is teaching a profession that has specific knowledge and research that develops over a career, or is teaching perhaps the work of a skilled craftsperson trained with a set of skills and techniques? What are teachers' core responsibilities, and to whom should they answer? Take a second to pause, reread, and think about these questions and how you would respond to them.

At first glance, these may appear to be rather basic questions; however, they on the contrary are not. Seemingly simple questions of purpose are in actuality full of incredible complexity and how we respond to them matters greatly. Broadly speaking, education as a discipline of study connects with and draws on a wide range of fields including, but not limited to, the social sciences, humanities, arts, biological sciences, business, and technology. And depending on who you ask there are many realities for exploring, interpreting, and imagining what education was, is, and might become. With so many nexuses, we do not perceive consensus exists in the answers to such questions; nor, do we necessarily consider total agreement possible, or even desirable. After all, if we are seeking to live more democratically as individuals and as societies, many voices are important to conversations on educational purposes.

Despite the lack of consensus regarding questions of the purposes, however, it is fair to say that almost all schools have well-established norms of policy and practice. Many of our educational institutions have also fashioned some sort of mission statement and/or a set of core values or goals. Stop and think about your school or a school you have been in before. *Can you recall what was the school's vision or mission? What about its values? Where did these come from, or what's the history behind them? Who determined them, and why? How are the educators working at your school embodying and/or resisting the mission and value? To what degree does your school embrace and encourage the values it professes? Moreover, how is your school embodying these? To what degree are the values democratic?*

Like each one of us, the educational institutions we inhabit are not blank slates. A lot has happened before we became part of them and more continues while we are a part of them. But when we are part of the flowing stream of goings-on, we can be like a fish that does not know the water in which it swims. Like a fish, we are organism immersed in environments with certain understandings of reality; we may not, however, always be able to perceive the greater whole we are living within and how we are contributing to. Our schools are always a cove in a must larger sea of educational currents. Professional awakening is about cultivating our perceptional awareness of the waters we are swimming in, while tuning our awareness toward what it means to become inspired educational professionals for democratic living.

CALLING OUT EDUCATION'S DOMINANT CULTURE

Most of us will readily observe that no two schools are alike. Think about any school you have been in or the one you are currently. If you are in North America, your school is likely part of a district, and your district is part of a network of other schools nested in a certain region of a state. And your state has neighboring states that are in turn part of a nation and globe. The point here is that any school's culture, even if not in the United States, is always nested in sets of relationships that are part of broader political, historical, socio-cultural contexts. And we need to enrich our understandings of these complexities. With such interconnectedness at play, there are habits, customs, and prevailing assumptions common to a dominant culture. Each one of us and our schools is naturally a part of the dominant culture, albeit in varying degrees.

Whether you are a pre-service teacher or an experienced educator, you have likely noticed that the guiding principles and theoretical platform introduced in this book dramatically differ from a lot of what is presently happening in so many schools be they public or private, kindergartens, middle schools, or high schools even universities. Our educational institutions and the structures established within them are reflections of our consciousness as human beings (Kumar, 2013), and the dominate culture of education fosters habituated reductionism linked to a management standardization. The dominant culture is by no means some sort of abstract theory rather one might think of it as a kind of substance that we as educators find ourselves living in daily. It is a sort of "thing" that gets absorbed into the very fabric of our minds, bodies, and hearts as educators.

We only need to take stock of what all we do and attend to on a daily basis to realize such standardized-management consciousness is at play. In fact, we encourage you to do just that here for a moment. Stop and create a list of what all you do (or might do) if you were in an educational setting. You might also want to consider what others do and say and what actions they take. All these little things we do and say each day turn into a week. Our weeks turn into months, and those months roll into years. Those years morph into decades and then into whole professional careers. What we feel, think, do, say, and make mirror to us ways in which the dominant culture becomes ingrained our individual and collective habits, discourses, and customs within and around schools.

To capture a sense of education's dominant culture's characteristics, an illustration may prove beneficial. The illustration below provides a general account of standardized-management consciousness in contrast with the wisdom-seeking consciousness at core of this book. Take a moment to examine the illustration. Again, we encourage you to pause and consider when and how you may have experienced any number of the traits listed.

Although this illustration points toward a sort of juxtaposition between two things, it is important to mention that what we present should not be interpreted as polar opposites. Dichotomies (e.g., right/wrong, science/mysticism, theory/practice, teacher/student) are at times helpful, but they can also become problematic when we think in strict, fixed either/or divisions. Thinking in such a way would mean that, for example, standards are bad or good. Or the individuals in schools are always operating from standardized-management consciousness and never with wisdom. To think in either/or terms is to reduce human experiences in the world to black and white and to not see the in-between spaces fill with shades of gray. A wisdom-seeking consciousness must live in the murky gray areas because it honors deliberations and the practice of critically informed judgments. At times, maybe establishing hierarchies or technical protocols using predetermined standards might be a wise

STANDARDIZED–MANAGEMENT CONSCIOUSNESS	WISDOM–SEEKING CONSCIOUSNESS
Power over and hierarchies	Power with/in and democratic collegiality
Reductionists, ranking, sorting	Holistic journeys of 3S understanding
Adhering to institutionalized understandings	Questioning authorities and habited practices
Ahistorical, short-term thinking	Historical, short/long-term thinking
Isolationism, control, fear, finger-pointing, scapegoating, righteousness	Collegial communities, freedom, vulnerability, agency, tact, humility, open-mindedness
Efficiency, top-down, coercive, orders, directives, compliance, neutrality, authoritarian	Choices, deliberative conversations, collegiality, caring, cooperation
Technical protocols	Trusting processes
Teachers as instructional technicians	Teachers as supreme artists
Decontextualized one-size-fits-all reforms	Contextualized, case-by-case negotiations
Rigidity, objectivity, separations, linearity	Flexibility, subjectivity, fluidity, recursive
Accountability through homogenous culture	Professional responsibility through embracing and honoring diverse voices

Figure 2.1. **Properties of Educational Consciousness**

judgement; at other times, perhaps these are not the most democratic ways of proceeding.

An important feature of professional awakening is that it encourages us to hold multiples in our mind at the same time. We can work toward a wisdom-seeking consciousness even when we are within a system governed by a pervasive standardized-management consciousness and the habituated ways of knowing and being it reinforces. We can seek to be generative learners with colleagues but still have to navigate teaching in a culture of testing. Professional awakening encourages us to strive for a balance. On the one hand, we must seek out ways to critically question and disrupt dominant structures and habits of thought in education, but we should not get lost and stay deconstructive. We, on the other hand, need to also work toward creatively reformulating opportunities to generate holistic understandings and invite others to do so too, which we will dig deeper into in the three folds to come.

Another vital aspect of professional awakening is that it rouses us to the felt qualities of becoming thoughtful democratic educators. Think back to a time when maybe you went to a doctor for a surgical procedure, or maybe to the dentist for a filling. Without doubt you were likely given some sort of anesthetic. If you have never had a surgery, perhaps you have taken some analgesics like a throat spray when ill or maybe a capsaicin cream for sore muscles. All anesthetics are substances that when absorbed into the body causes a numbness. A person loses sensations, sometimes even consciousness, to the world around them and to her/his own interiority. This brings us to another deeply concerning consequence of the dominant culture promoted by standardized management consciousness, which is it acts as an anesthetic in our lives as educators and in our students' lives.

The dominant culture anesthetizes us to our inner thoughts, feelings, imaginations, and creativity, while a certain ethos is promoted including desires to: (a) control and predict, (b) compare and contrast, (c) use extrinsic motivations, (d) demand clear, specific outcomes, and (e) use measurements to evaluate performance (Eisner, 2001). Because of these we may end up silencing ourselves because we feel no one will care or listen. Or we may keep quiet because we want to keep our jobs, fearing that if we speak up some backlash may happen. We may even take to closing our classroom doors as attempts to create spaces that we feel do not "fit" with the norms. Worse yet, we may find ourselves turning into bureaucratic sleepwalkers simply going through the motions, doing this or that to simply finish another form or check a box. When professional practices get their meaning purely from external structures, educators can quickly lose sight of what brought them to the professional in the first place. We can end up entering a sort of standardization–slumber that feeds and wants to maintain habits for narrow reflective inquiry, hierarchies of authority, and bureaucratic image of curriculum and pedagogy

Let us dig a little deeper into the anesthetic through the current trends toward increasingly standardized education. Christopher Tienken's (2017) work is helpful for parsing out some qualities in standardized education; put another way, we have grown accustomed to a particular theoretical orientation that often goes unnoticed, unmentioned, and unexamined. To shed critical light on this implicit theorizing, most of the educational policy and practices in the United States are informed by what Tienken calls, performativity theory. Performativity refers to how we communicate, act, react, enact, and construct identities in standardized teaching-learning environments. What this means in education is that certain ways of thinking and being are supported, including: "extreme behaviorism, the Essentialist philosophy of education, linguistic relativism, the Cult of Specificity, and an unyielding belief in [an autocratic] meritocracy" (p. 79). Each one of Tienken's five criteria is worth unpacking and illustrating because they can help further with painting a picture around the fatally flawed foundation of standardized education. First, we understand and define his terms as follows:

- *Behaviorism* is a psychological approach for measuring knowledge through observed behavioral stimuli and responses. Extreme behaviorism has a narrow, rigid focus on selected, predetermined behavioral changes in an environment. Such behaviorism emphasizes standardized surveillance, measurement, prediction, and control.
- *Essentialism* is a philosophy of education that assumes there is a common, essential set of knowledge that everyone needs for a quality life; students need to acquire this knowledge to be productive members of society.
- *Linguistic relativism* points our attention to how all discourse carries and expresses meanings. The language, words, phrases, and rhetoric we use every day to communicate verbally and in texts can be used without deep thought being given to what it is we say and do.
- *Cult of Specificity* refers to the proclivity for precise, literal answers with detriment to nuances. Two key metaphors capture the spirit of this include: "losing sight of the forest for the trees" and "seeing black and white, not shades of gray."
- *Belief in an autocratic meritocracy* is the idea that there are authorities in education who have the answers about what "works." Their judgments are seen as the truth; they do not need to engage in democratic deliberations.

Now, let us turn our attention to a variety of ways in which these criteria are often reified in schools. Performativity is tied to learning outcomes of the standardized-management consciousness, which have become routine aspects of teacher's daily practice. Common Core curricular standards, dictate learning outcomes from a centralized authority that are uniform across most states. Even in international many contexts ministries of education have pre-determined content. The prevalent assumption that a predetermined set of particular learning outcomes represent college or career readiness epitomizes Essentialist philosophy. The unquestioned presumption is that there is fixed set of knowledge, skills, and dispositions, which are essential to all students' future success or competency.

Correspondingly, the language and rhetoric commonly used in schools and around education often goes on unexamined. Yet what we say is influential to the ways we think and make important educational decisions. Differentiating instruction, having high standards, as well as being inclusive and culturally responsive are regularly used in seemingly unobjectionable ways; but, to what degree are the phrases and words we take up and use in education simply bandwagons, doublespeak, or hollow promises? Descriptions of children with reference to "being on grade level" and appraisals of teacher effectiveness in terms of "value added" influence teachers to conceive of learning processes as a linear and predictable trajectory of measurable progress. Within the pervasive discourse of essentialism and behaviorism, classrooms become allegedly meritorious, cults of specificity, narrowly acknowledging and rewarding only expressions of understanding that demonstrate the "I can . . ." statement posted before class on the chalkboard.

Today, schools seem to be prefaced with the phrase, "performance-based," and performativity can be see in everyday language that get tossed around like: Are young children kindergarten ready? As they proceed to elementary school, are they reading on grade level? Then, in high school, are they college and career ready? While common sense might be telling us, "Of course we want students and teachers to perform well!" performance is not a benign concept. Indeed, schools are increasingly demanding particular sorts of performances on specified timelines. Teachers' effectiveness is appraised with reference to students' learning trajectory, as well as their own adherence to instructional behaviors specified on observational rubrics. Behaviorism is upheld through systematic rating systems and to some degree everyone is being watched. Rituals of surveillance are commonly undertaken through progress monitoring tests (for students) and administrative walkthroughs (for teachers), valuing conformity and infusing the gaze of authority on the process of knowledge acquisition.

All of this is based on the assumption that there is a uniform set of essential knowledge and skills and a predictable trajectory of what an educated person knows, understands, and is able to do. Educators often reference these notions of readiness with such a strong focus on specific measureable outcomes, but they often overlook the complexity and ambiguity of what it means to "be ready" for life's next undertaking. Yet, we often presumptively discuss what constitutes good schools, good teachers, and good students without any deep consideration of alternative interpretations of curriculum, teaching, and leadership. In effect, performativity and its various manifestations are metaphorical sleeping pills many educators do not realize they have taken. The professional awakening fold challenges us to be less presumptuous and critically question what we do and why with reference to democratic values.

In the dominant culture, educational vocations can get reduced to superficial terms. Predetermined definitions of achievement suppress the infinite potential outcomes of educational experience and promulgating performances of compliance and uniformity. Does this common version of schooling even qualify as an educational experience? Or, is it something else? Instead of presuming that coming to school ought to result in shared understandings, professional awakening signals toward the possibility of educational experience for making its participants (students and teachers) more distinct. An imperative for cultivating a democratic problem-solving artistry among educators is to draw on an internal drive from within *good-hearted, open-minded, and responsible* teachers. If we, as teachers, do not remain connected to a vocational sense of agency and critically question the socio-moral purposes underlying our professional activities, than the status quo discourses and practices ascribe meaning to our curriculum and pedagogy.

Professional awakening is not only about becoming critical of the dominant culture but also about turning the critical lens back on yourself. We have to be radically honest within ourselves about the degree to which we are being good-hearted, open-minded, and responsible pedagogical artists. Such honesty will likely challenge our comfort zones. Who we think we are and what we think is true will be brought into question. One way of beginning is to become an honest observer of yourself. Call into question your own thoughts, actions, and reactions as well as explore the situations you find yourself in. That is right, blow the whistle on yourself! Work on calling yourself out on yourself. Endless examples and possibilities of this exist. As examples, do you believe that all students' voices matter in school but does your school not have faculty support for an LGBTQIA student organization when students' self-identify as such? Do you believe you are open-minded but when colleagues share their experiences you silently roll your eyes and in your mind say "Uh, yeah right. You have no idea what you are talking about"? Blow your own cover and catch when what you are saying and doing do not match up.

Although they can be, learning through experiences is not always pleasant, and the added dimension of living democratically in our societies and classrooms is a further challenge to our inner growth and values. An important part of our journeys of understanding though is not to get stuck in an endless cycle of feeling shame or like a failure. Do, however, stop and acknowledge where and when your beliefs, thoughts, and action fall out of balance. Doing this can aid in bringing to your awareness areas of exploration around who you are personally and professionally as well as propelling you forward to taking different actions. Who is it you believe you are as an educator? Who is it you want to be and become? Also, be kind to yourself because there is no set way in which professional awakening occurs. Perhaps you are hesitant about the ideas for democratic values. Or perhaps you resonate with certain ideas. We highly encourage you to reflect on your thoughts and feelings. Remember that being, becoming, and embodying democracy as a way of living is *a practice* full of tensions and joys, steps forward and steps backward, clarity, and uncertainty. Practical wisdom embraces a journey of understanding that is humble and evolving rather than a fixed path to mastery.

A DELIBERATIVE CONVERSATION

Because the dialogues we have with one another can be illuminating, to further illustrate the ideas we have been discussing thus far about professional awakening, we have decided to recount and creatively compile conversations we have had in our everyday lives with fellow educators over the years. The purpose of these hypothetical dialogues, which happen in each fold, is threefold. One, we are attempting to model how one might go about inviting dialogue with educational stakeholders. Two, we are trying to call attention to the importance of being reflective in multiple ways and working toward deliberative conversations around democratic virtues. Three, we wanted to capture some of the common characteristics around the educational problem solving that happens in contemporary schools. As authors, we participate in these dialogues with two imagined, hardworking colleagues named, Dorothy and Cindy.

To set the stage for our deliberative conversation, we want to introduce you to our two colleagues. Dorothy is a public school principal with over 30 years of experience who now works in a College of Education, focusing on principal preparation. She often dismisses the utility of theorizing, explaining that her concern is with practice. Dorothy is a respected educator with a jovial personality, excellent organizational skills, and quick to offer words of encouragement and advice. Cindy is a highly experienced teacher, instructional coach, and currently teaches various literacy courses to preservice and practicing

teachers at the same College of Education as Dorothy. Cindy is more recep-
tive to educational theorizing than Dorothy, though Cindy might explain there
are limits to how "philosophical" she gets in her own endeavors. Like Dorothy, she too has an impressive work ethic and is known in her professional
communities for being an outstanding educator. Also, like Dorothy, Cindy's
efforts are attentive to educators' daily practices; however, Cindy's focus is
on "bridging" an alleged "chasm between theory and practice." Hence, Cindy
regularly attends state- and national-level professional organizations' conferences and enthusiastically promulgates "research-based best practices" among
teachers. As we enter into this imaginary dialogue, you will likely be reminded
of comments commonly made by classroom teachers, educational administrators, and professors in colleges of education. Dan gets the conversation started
with an invitation to deliberate about educational purposes.

> **Dan:** *Dorothy, I'm wondering if you have considered incorporating a curricu-
> lum course, or maybe two, into the principal preparation program here at the
> university? It might enrich principals' educational understandings.*

> **Dorothy:** *Ya know, I don't see any real purpose or value for having a course, or
> courses, on curriculum in our educational leadership and administration program.*

> **Dan:** *Hmm, why is that?*

> **Dorothy:** *School leaders are reasonably intelligent people, and they know what
> needs to be taught in their schools. Standards, pacing guides, program materi-
> als . . . all of the curriculum is really given to a principal by the district, and
> any district will have their directives from the state and federal levels. Plus, the
> superintendents know and understand the curriculum that's given to schools.
> As the leaders, they have too many other things they need to worry about and
> do not need to be to spending too much time and energy on curriculum. They
> need to be focused on making sure all of their teachers are on the same page
> regarding the curriculum. In our program, we need to focus on developing good
> school leaders with management skills. Good leaders know how to monitor their
> teachers and make sure they are working in unison. Good leaders know that
> sometimes in order to get teachers on same page some support structures might
> need to be put into place to help out like subject area coaches maybe curriculum
> specialists or consultants.*

> **Jen:** *Well, I'm wondering about the aims of our college's educational leader
> program though, especially given how we proclaim to be invested in fostering
> democratic values within our program and our graduates. Aspiring principals
> could be introduced to and begin practicing a more holistic view of leadership
> through our program. Perhaps, we can approach our curriculum through a vi-
> sion that intertwines curriculum with leadership and teaching as well as having
> an attentiveness to students and learning? There's a lot of interconnectedness at
> play, and it seems to me that our programs should attune and encourage educa-*

tional leaders to cultivate understandings of the many complexities and layers that are present in education. Educational studies is rich with relationships and ethical concerns in need of serious deliberation.

Jim: *Ethics is a very important consideration for all of us as educators. Do you think building principals and other school leaders understand the important influence they have as curriculum leaders? For example, we have theorized a fourfold problem-solving process that highlights four different forms of critical thinking. Of course, we would all agree that we want our schools' principals to be strong critical thinkers and leaders.*

Dorothy: *I'm sure that is really great stuff, but to me it is just for the talking heads at academic conferences. Academics are off in their ivory towers thinking all the time and not in the real world of schools and what goes on. I'm not overly interested in getting lost in what the talking heads write in their journals or what they are discuss at their conferences. I was a principal for 30 years and it is a lot of hard work each and every day. These new principals need to know what they are going to be expected to do on day one. They need to have their toolboxes full as soon as they start the job, and it's our jobs in the program to give those tools to them. No one cares if they know all of theory. Theory doesn't have much to do with what happens every day as good school leaders.*

Cindy: *I think my perspective is somewhere in between. I agree with Dorothy that school leaders need to know what to do, but at the end of the day, the most important thing that happens at schools is teaching and learning. How are we helping our principals promote best practices in every classroom? That's an important question we need to always be asking ourselves, and that is where I think curriculum is important and comes together with leadership. It's all about instruction. One thing that good principals need to know on their first day is how to recognize research-based best practices, when they are and when they are not seeing them in classrooms. From my experience, curriculum design is a big part of that. Don't we want our principals to be able to lead PLCs [professional learning communities] where teachers are creating good constructivist lessons and units? A good leader's primary job is to ensure that there is excellent instruction in every classroom because all our students deserve this.*

Dorothy: *Well, it all depends. The purpose of education is to raise student achievement, which is measured on standardized tests, whether we like that or not. I know we should not always teach to the test, but we need data from those test to identify what our problem areas even are with teachers' instruction and students' learning. What you are talking about, Cindy, might hold true for some higher performing districts that aren't under the gun from the state, when it comes to testing data. But there are a lot of schools out there that don't have the time to worry about whether or not their lessons are constructivist or not. They need to focus on data because it can tell us what's happening and how things are improving or not. Besides, when you are a principal, you better believe your district administrators are going to be paying attention to that data. They know* *what the school's problems are, and they expect principals to get results. When it comes to curriculum, principals usually have their marching orders and they are going to be expecting their teachers to be following the curriculum guides. If you venture too far astray, you are going to get yourself into trouble. When you are the leader, you've gotta keep all of your little ducks in a row.*

UNPACKING THE COLLEGIAL EXCHANGE

As readers, you have likely encountered comments similar to those expressed by Dorothy and Cindy. Or perhaps you recall in certain educational conversations having said similar things as Dorothy and Cindy. Let us unpack some of what has transpired in the conversation. Firstly, Dorothy and Cindy showcase, for us, commonly held views about education that stand in contrast to the problem-solving artistry advanced in this book. Their remarks are framed by the two most pervasive sets of paradigmatic assumptions used in educational problem solving (Henderson & Gornik, 2007). Specifically, Dorothy serves as an embodiment of the standardized management of instruction. Cindy, on the other hand, exemplifies a constructivist best practice orientation. Although in many ways their points of view contrast with ours as well as with each other's, our intentions here are not to devalue their viewpoints and dedication as educators. None of the conversations found in these folds is an attempt to win an argument. Rather, we are trying to demonstrate the sort of humble, respectful collegial inviting and the deliberative conversations anchoring this book's problem solving.

From the exchange above, we can also glimpse how Dorothy's and Cindy's interpretations of educational problem-solving contrasts with the vision we are advancing in this book. In two different ways, Dorothy and Cindy express the very common interpretations of Tyler's rationale. However, since Tyler's four-part procedure has been the predominant approach to curriculum development for over half a century now, they utilized it without conscientiously referencing Tyler or his four fundamental questions. It can be said then that habituated patterns of problem solving are woven into the fabric of their minds and actions. So much so that Dorothy does not appear to recognize that she too is engaged with curricular decisions.

Both of our colleagues also seem to be anesthetized to the existential qualities of their journeys. They are appealing to external authorities for validation instead of a sense of moral agency within themselves. Thinking back to the seven guiding principles in chapter 1, Dorothy and Cindy are exhibiting a sense of educational accountability but not so much educational responsibility, which was a critical distinction from Nel Noddings (2013). Dorothy and

Cindy animate for us understandings of a sort of compliance-based, professional ethic of educational practice. For Dorothy, she presumes *good* educational leaders restore law and uphold order in an otherwise chaotic situation. Conceptualized as a problem of law and order, she sets out to get everyone on the same page and be obedient to a universal, authoritative plan. Cindy, on the other hand, presumes that she has found the truth of what is good from "best practices," or put another way, what the research tells us works; Cindy simply needs to take this research and spread the good news far and wide to fellow colleagues.

The two common discourses that Dorothy and Cindy are using are extremely problematic. With a value-neutral facade, educators like Dorothy and Cindy are actually, albeit inadvertently, adhering to ideological structures that reproduce social inequalities. Whether conserving institutional order or promulgating a unified visions of professional best practices, our conversation partners express interpretations of educational practice understood within the boundaries of extant structures of authority. Contrastively informed by critical theories, various educators view curriculum and pedagogy as an activity with revolutionary potential for overturning the established orders articulated and reinforced by Dorothy and Cindy. Although critical educators have shed important light on how power subtly operates through the most taken for granted enactments of educational discourse and practices, the esoteric jargon of critical theories remains much more prominent in the academic circles than in K-12 schools and policies. Moreover, in their zeal to confront, contest, and overturn conservative ideology, critical educators run the risk of perpetuating a counter ideology of their own.

Professional awakening—and the overall problem-solving scaffolding in this book—strives to put forth a process for democratic relations, instead of ideological adherence. Education in a freedom-loving society calls for good-hearted, open-minded, responsible judgments of intrinsically motivated, autonomous professionals. Instead of external structures of authority the discipline from within one's vocational calling ought to power educational problem solving. Our responses to Dorothy and Cindy, therefore, are cautious of being an abrasive critique nor do we completely reject or dismiss their ideas. Rather, we would hope to express ourselves in ways that respects their diligence and honors their good intentions. At the same time, however, we are mindful that the path to hell is paved with good intentions, and we share the serious concerns and questions raised by critical educators.

In the deliberative conversation, we (Jim, Jen, and Dan) are butting up against and challenging deeply held values that have become embedded in the habits of American educators. Dorothy and Cindy are commitment educators who exemplify certain habituated values of American schooling. The

values referred to here are static or regressive in nature and point only to specific, technical dimensions of teaching. From a technical view of education,
problem solving is more often than not initiated by clearly stating a learning
objective(s). Articulated either as observable behaviors or as subject-centered
goals, the desired outcomes can be prefaced with the phrase, "Students will
be able to . . ." The habit within schools is to value predetermined standards
and orient educators problem solving around "craft reflection" with questions
like: How can we most efficiently and/or effectively ensure that students
learn these prescribed standards? Moreover, the problems adhere to a systematic view of curriculum. How can we ensure that students are learning
what authority figures has deemed essential for them to be learning at this
particular stage of their education?

Trying to open space for professional awakening, we are attempted to encourage Dorothy and Cindy to engage in multiple forms of reflective inquiry through
deliberative conversations. In effect, we were trying to get our colleagues to
consider democratically progressive values attuned to not only the technical
features but also the value-laden aspects of teaching. Seeking to engage in aims
talking with a focuses on how educational activities are connected to central
aims of life is our attempt to broaden and deepen Dorothy and Cindy's technical
approach to educational problem solving. Aims talking raises questions about
beliefs and practices while provoking careful consider of: "Why are we proceeding as we are?" and "How does this particular course of action bring us closer
to democratic virtues?" Certainly, there are technical ends, emphasizing what
"students will be able to," but these specific objectives are need to be integrated
into a broader conversation about their potential enduring values to students and
societies. Let us pause for a moment and consider the following questions.

• *What might you say if you were just now joining our conversation with
  Dorothy and Cindy about interpretations of educational purposes?*

• *How might we encourage Dorothy and Cindy to engage in more democratically informed conversations about educational problem solving?
  How might we tap into a sense of historical agency, inviting them to invoke
  their vocational callings and a range of voices into the conversation?*

A wisdom-seeking consciousness finds it necessary to truthfully express
our skepticism regarding the progress that can be achieved by perpetuating
the dominant educational discourse-practices. There are indeed a number
of very undemocratic traditions and habits that have been developed over
the history of American schooling. Take as examples, how eugenics made
its way into education through classifying the intelligence of students from

racial groups and sorting their abilities and social worth accordingly (Winfield, 2007), or the dehumanization of Native peoples whose cultures were de-legitimized by the United States' federal government through the use of education and boarding schools (Adams, 1995; Child, 2000). Our stance is that disrupting those habits and dismantling the structures of those traditions is vital but only one side of the coin. The other side is hopeful and pragmatic. Curriculum—structured through the interrelated activities of teaching and leading—is both a complicated conversation and an existential journey of pivotal importance. In such conversations, authentic and autonomous participants are necessarily for deliberations about educational problems especially when working in a society that professes democratic aspirations.

An unfortunate consequences of standardized-management consciousness is that is has an anesthetic, de-intellectualizing, and conforming effects on educational professionals. This does not, however, mean that teachers and administrators are uncaring, unintelligent, or unmotivated in their efforts to educate new generations. Rather, we assume quite the opposite. It is our assumption that awakening educators to professional artistry opens up possibilities for perhaps the most underutilized resource in American education: the contextual and deeply personal knowledge and commitments of dedicated educators. Teachers' insights are derived from the experiences of being in direct contact with students, families, and communities. Teachers' qualitative understandings cannot be replicated by distal authorities and deserve appreciation and serious consideration in educational conversations and decisions. We assert that professional educators, particularly teachers, possess irreplaceable potential for enhancing schools. Regrettably, for over a century, the dominant policy environment has sought to micromanage educators, instead of encouraging and supporting them to develop their professional artistry.

PARTING THOUGHTS

At the heart of the professional awakening fold is the question: What constitutes the aims of a *good* education? Even though we reside in the dominant culture that does not mean we have to belong to it or fully agree with it. Professional awakening asks us to be courageous. Have courage to look around and ask hard questions about our schools and the societies we are living. Be courageous to look inward at yourselves and examine your beliefs, thoughts, and feelings about education.

Turn on your inner observer, check your motives, and ask yourselves hard questions about who you think you are as educators and how you have become who you are. And who is it you want to continue being, or what kind of educator might you want to become? Perhaps you are hesitant about democratic values in schools, why? Or perhaps you fully embrace democratic values, but do you do so dogmatically? How often do you engage in deliberations about democratic values with other educational stakeholders? Of utmost importance is to remember that there is no perfect, predetermined, controllable way in which professional awakening occurs; we each come to our own understandings of becoming professional artists in our own ways and in our own time.

Pause and Ponder

An crucial part of the fourfold process, and each fold with it, is to make the time to pause and really take stock of how things are going. To help get you started, here are some questions to consider, but please know these are by no means an exhaustive set of questions. These are simple to get you started.

- Professional awakening asks us to each get in touch base with our sense identity as educators and how our identity has been cultivated over time. Who is it we think we are, and what is it we believe? How did we come to identify with certain ideas and ideals about education? Ask yourself: Why did I become an educator? What is it I am thinking and feeling as a professional teacher in the twenty-first century?
- How am I doing with raising my *awareness* of the *knowledge-power relations* that structure educational practices, decisions, and policies?
- What sorts of conversations have I had with colleagues around educational purposes? What might have been some of the personal and socio-cultural dynamics at play in those conversations?
- How am I finding ways to rekindle and nurture my *professional being* as an educator?
- How am I doing with making sense of and embodying what it means to be *an open-minded, generous, and generative democratic educator*?

DELVING DEEPER: STUDY RESOURCES

To close out each fold, we want to end by sharing offerings with you. Our offerings are collections of resources that we have found helpful in stretching our thinking about the fold at hand. Even though the authors of these resources do not use the folds per say, their writings have enriched our understandings in different ways. And so, we leave you with a set around professional awakening below and invite you to consider materials you have encountered that may help you make connections to the ideas in this book.

Palmer, P. (2007). *The Courage to teach: Exploring the inner landscape of a teacher's life.* San Francisco, CA: Jossey-Bass.

This book is very supportive in term of beginning to think about how our teacher being is all at once intellectual, emotional, and spiritual, and how we need to find ways to, as Parker Palmer says, "deepen, renew, and sustain" our sense of professional "vocation in trying times" (p. xiv).

Intrator, S. M., & Scribner, M. (2003). *Teaching with fire: Poetry that sustains the courage to teach.* San Francisco, CA: Jossey-Bass.
Intrator, S. M., & Scribner, M. (2014). *Teaching with heart: Poetry that speak to the courage to teach.* San Francisco, CA: Jossey-Bass.

In both books, Sam Intrator and Megan Scribner blend poetry with educators' personal reflections and evoke a sense of a multi-vocal conversation around educational purposes. The books touch on the theme of how the contemporary conditions are impacting teachers' creativity, autonomy, and expertise. But this is coupled with stories educators share regarding their passions, commitment to the call to teach, and enduring meaning of being educators.

Ayers, W. (2010). *To teach: The journey of a teacher.* New York, NY: Teachers College Press.

William (Bill) Ayers's book, which comes in both a narrative form as well as in a graphic novel form, follows the story of one teacher's journey into the ethical, intellectual, and emotional dimensions of being an educator. The book is a powerful illustration that captures many of the challenges and aspirations in our fourfold process and conceptual platform.

Hansen, D. (1995). *The call to teach.* New York, NY: Teachers College Press.

David Hansen's book in an exploration of vocational calling coupled with research into the everyday lived experiences of teachers. Hansen invites us to consider the relationship between our personal lives and professional practice, our values and beliefs about teaching, our tensions and desires, and much more.

Pirsig, R. (1974). *Zen and the art of motorcycle maintenance: Inquiry into Values.* New York, NY: HarperCollins Publishers.

Although not focused on education *per se*, this is a thought-provoking book about the notion of a journey of understanding. Robert Pirsig engages us in examining how it is we are living in the world, and how we might live better together in the world.

Block, A. A. (2008). Why should I be a teacher? *Journal of Teacher Education 9*(5), 416–27.

Alan Block is a curriculum theorist who writes with wit and candor. In this article, Block reflects on his own experiences as an educator and teacher educator. He accounts for many of the joys and challenges inherent to being a teacher.

REFERENCES

Adams, D. W. (1995). *Education for extinction: American Indians and the boarding school experience, 1875–1928.* Lawrence, KS: University Press of Kansas.

Child, B. J. (2000). *Boarding school seasons: American Indian families, 1900–1940.* Lincoln, NE: University of Nebraska Press.

Eisner, E. W. (2001). What does it mean to say a school is doing well? *Phi Delta Kappa, 82*(2), 367–72.

Henderson, J. G., & Gornik, R. (2007). *Transformative curriculum leadership* (3rd ed.). Upper Saddle River, NJ: Merrill/Prentice Hall.

Kumar, A. (2013). *Curriculum as meditative inquiry.* New York, NY: Palgrave Macmillan.

Noddings, N. (2013). *Education and democracy in the 21st century.* New York, NY: Teachers College Press.

Tienken, C. H. (2017). *Defying Standardization: Creating curriculum for an uncertain future.* Lanham, MD: Rowman & Littlefield.

Winfield, A. G. (2007). *Eugenics and education in America: Institutionalized racism and the implications of history, ideology, and memory.* New York, NY: Peter Lang Publishing.

Chapter Three

Holistic Teaching

How are we experiencing the transactional artistry of teaching for students' subject understandings deepened by democratic self and social understandings?

All of our schools and classrooms are sites where teaching and learning transpire, but what sort of educational spaces are we cultivating in our classrooms? What is the nature of the educational experiences that occur? What does it mean to teach? What does it mean to learn? How might these questions be understood from the vantage points of a teacher or a student? What are the enduring values of the educational experiences in our classrooms? The holistic teaching fold, in brief, beckons us to consider such questions and enriching our understandings of holistic, democratic education as teachers as well as encouraging students' journeys of holistic understanding. As we pointed out in the professional awakening fold, educational problem solving frequently encourages certain habituated roles, expectations, responsibilities, and behaviors. These habits and customs extend into our classroom and the relationships we have with our students.

Think back to the professional awakening fold's discussion alongside the table dedicated to educational consciousness in which we distinguished some of the general properties of a standardized-management consciousness and a wisdom-seeking consciousness. Although those ideas when written down appear to "live" in a separate chapter, they actually do not and fold into this chapter. Remember that while there may appear to be boundaries in this book, the fourfold process is highly porous. Therefore, we encourage you to going back and forth and build connections between the ideas expressed in the fourfolds. Educational purposes and educational experiences are enmeshed. Through educational experiences we not only experienced subject matter, but "we [also] learn ways to be and these ways, perhaps more than cognitive learning, stay with us throughout our lives" (Blumenfeld-Jones, 2012, p. 29). This observation about educational experiences is particularly important for us to remember.

- How would teaching and learning look/feel if we removed an individual's *self-understanding* and *self-reflection* from educational experiences?
- What would teaching and learning look/feel like if we removed *social understandings* from educational experiences?
- What would teaching and learning look/feel like if we removed *democratic values* from educational experiences? What might living in the world be like if we eliminated them?

To begin our description of the general nature of holistic teaching, we continue in a comparative spirit in order to help situated the rest of this chapter for you.

The image below attempts to visualize a common, habitual flow of teaching and learning that happens in so many K-12 educational contexts today, even in higher education. While there can certainly be degrees of variation, the general flow within standardized experiencing proceeds as such. A teacher typically plans educational experiences organized around predetermined standard(s) that are part of a pre-given curriculum from an authority figure. A teacher then instructs via some sort of lesson/unit, this is, the distribution of curriculum to the students. Students are the individuals who experience the learning of the subject matter, and at some point, all the students produce some kind of observable performative outcome. The outcome is given to the teacher who in turn assesses the outcome. With this way of being in the

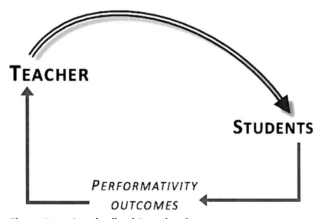

Figure 3.1.   Standardized Experiencing

classroom, at the end of the day, the teacher decides and assesses how and if students have demonstrated learning of the content. Once teacher assesses the outcome, students receive grades or marks on the quality of their work. The cycle continues as such over and over again.

As you will recall from the professional awakening fold, performativity shapes how we communicate, act, react, enact, and construct identities. When standardized experiencing underlays our teaching and learning environments, performativity is abundant and thrives. Critically examining such standardized experiencing reveals habituated roles, responsibilities, behaviors, and customs we seem to cling to in our pedagogies. There is an endless collection of examples, and it is likely you even have some in your own mind as well.

An example of performativity germane to educational practices is that common content standards are routinely transfigured into behavioral objectives. With such static uniformity of purpose, rigid structures often confine possibilities for classroom experiences. Another example is how subjects are often structured and taught as separate from each other. When was the last time you experienced a melding of subject areas or an interdisciplinary or multidisciplinary classroom? The ways we think about and treat educational experiences in our classrooms has impacts. Educational experiences reinforce to us and to students, "what knowledge is [considered] worthwhile" and "what is worth . . . experiencing, doing, needing, being, becoming, overcoming, sharing, and contributing" (Schubert, 2010, p. 235).

Anywhere from commonplace scope and sequence charts to highly restrictive scripted and mapped-out instruction, trends toward standardization stifle pedagogical artistry. Under the assumption that the boxed curriculum contains content essential to students' future well-being, educators dutifully maintain fidelity to a program, initiative, or practice. In doing so, we unwittingly function as semi-professional, and we also unknowingly and uncritically reproducing static or even regressive values. In effect, if the organizing purpose of schooling is to improve student achievement on standardized content and test, teachers' and students' educational experiences will also embody standardized and bureaucratic qualities.

In chapter 3, however, we advanced professional awakening as a more expansive alternative to standardized educational purposes. If the aims of education are instead organized around evolving, freedom loving, justice-oriented existential journeys and democratic aspirations, standardized experiences do not suffice. Professional artistry and journeys of holistic, democratic understanding honor idiocracies and individuals' freedom "from within," while standardization focuses on making something or someone the same. Standardization finds ways of conforming the world and us to particular measures, which can have dehumanizing effects. If the square peg does not fit in the round hole, we find ways to make it, or at least we try. With these ideas in mind, let us now bring in a contrasting teaching-learning image for contemplation.

Holistic teaching is about embracing and supporting transactional experiencing in our classrooms and schools. The visual representation of transactional experiencing above is an attempt to showcase a different sort of educational experiencing that stands in vivid contrast to standardized teaching and learning environments. Our image above attempts to visually represent, in a distilled form, the dynamic, flowing nature of teaching-learning when informed by the sensibilities of a wisdom-seeking consciousness. When classrooms embrace transactional experiencing, we seek ways to disrupt and dislodges practices that are universal, unidirectional, and linear. Transaction unites teaching and learning, which we try to represent here in writing by using a hyphen. That is, there is an interplay and interdependence between teaching and learning. Teacher and students also merge in a sort of swirling vortex in which they teach-learn from and with one another.

Many educators already on an intuitive level infuse such transactional artistry into their daily practices. They do problem solving daily that advances democratic values and case-by-case deliberations with students. Transactional teachers are careful listeners, and they value the authentic expressions of diverse journeys of understanding. Many teachers consider themselves to be "lifelong learners." To be clear, we are not endorsing an anything-goes

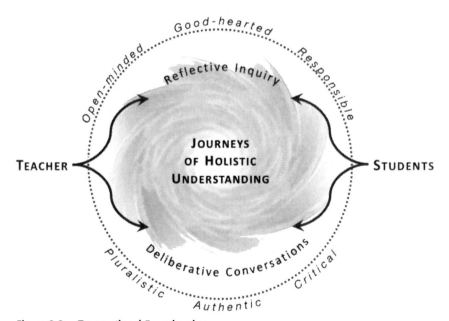

Figure 3.2. Transactional Experiencing

approach to teaching with transactional artistry. To the contrary, creative teachers set out to embody values such as criticality, cooperation, civility, and humility in their daily practices. In doing so, creative teachers are attempting to cultivate their own and students' authentic participation in rigorous learning tasks. With authentic participation personal experiences and social contexts are integrated into the process of academic study.

Worth doing here is for us to look back at the theoretical underpinnings of the holistic teaching that were discussed in our chapter 1 platform. This book is inspired and informed by the great American educational philosopher, John Dewey as well as the curriculum theorist, Elliot Eisner. Teaching is always and inevitably laced with theory. Colleagues, like Dorothy and Cindy, would be pleased to hear that Dewey and Eisner were pragmatic thinkers, involved in theorizing out of an interest in improving daily practices and not for the sake of esoteric abstractions. Dewey, against the grain of his time, argued that teaching was not exclusively a science but also properly understood as an art. To be more exact, the supreme art in societies with democratic aspirations.

In part by drawing on his background in the arts, Eisner entered the picture sometime later. Eisner took up and more thoroughly theorized Dewey's conceptualizations of pedagogical artistry. Amid his career and prolific writing, this passage nicely captures Eisner's sense of teaching artistry.

> Teaching can be done as badly as anything else. It can be wooden, mechanical, mindless, and wholly unimaginative. But when it is sensitive, intelligent and creative—those qualities that confer upon it the status of an art—it should . . . not be regarded, as it so often is by some, as an expression of unfathomable talent or luck but as an example of humans exercising the highest levels of their intelligence. (Eisner, 1994, pp. 154–56)

The art of teaching that Eisner is gesturing toward in his descriptive words has certain dimensions. Artistry is sensitive to and nurtures certain properties in our pedagogies: grace, intelligence, creativity; judgements about teaching-learning qualities happen in real-time moment by moment; the ends of teaching-learning can be emergent in nature and often created through experience; a balance between "automaticity and inventiveness" or put another way routine and creativity (p. 135). Picking up on Dewey and Eisner, we too want to consider what it might mean to be an awakening professional educator—that is, one who is attempting to enact teaching practices that are creative, imaginative, and expressive and infused with deepening democratic self and social understandings.

Holistic teaching builds on the professional awakening we discussed in the chapter prior. Drawing on our powers to be critical, imaginative autonomously thinking and inquisitive teachers, holistic teaching is a very concrete and practical action. And in a sense, holistic teaching has two parts: the activating of a teacher's vocational calling and the cultivating of students' holistic, 3S understandings. Teachers and students enjoy relationships of reciprocity that are mutually beneficial. Professionally awakened teachers find themselves on humble journeys of understanding that evolve over the course of their careers.

Such teachers love to broaden their personal and professional horizons with new learning, and they see possibilities in their schools and classrooms becoming sites for professional development. These teachers always find themselves learning from and with their students. They are intrinsically motivated to engage in reflective inquiry and deliberative conversations in ways that embrace the complexities and ambiguities of teaching. This embrace in turn shapes their classroom and students' experiences. Put differently, teachers who are on their own journeys of holistic understandings open up spaces for the emergence of opportunities for students to embark on their own journeys of holistic understanding.

A DELIBERATIVE CONVERSATION

We want to return to our hypothetical dialogue with our colleagues, Dorothy and Cindy. Their remarks show us that they are engaged in a certain form of educational problem solving implicitly anchored in Ralph Tyler's (1949) imperishable questions on purpose, experience, organization, and evaluation. This might be understood as the general strength in their thinking and work, and it to a certain degree is their common ground with us. Although do not forget we are pushing against the rigid ideologies of vulgar pragmatism, value-neutral, and technical tendencies of Tyler's rationale. There is a more specific element in Dorothy's and Cindy's approaches to discussing education that is perhaps even more praiseworthy and another point of entry to dialogue. They each have deeply held commitments to focus on improving teaching practice and believe that teaching and learning are connected. We share Dorothy's, Cindy's, and others colleagues' interest in improving daily pedagogical practices. Furthermore, we deeply value the pragmatic utility of theory for such efforts.

In our prior conversation though, recall that Dorothy expressed an atheoretical stance, failing to see the relevance of theory in the practical affairs of educational leaders. Cindy, on the other hand, seemed to express more interest in theory. From her point of view, theory and research are relevant authoritative voices for finding the "right answers" for education. As Cindy sees it, her job is akin to being a translator of sorts; that is, she is making sure that teachers know and understand what the expertise and research say.

Educational leadership is all about this: building teachers capacity, spreading research-based practices, and ensuring these best practice are being utilized in every classroom. As our attention in our collegial dialogue shifts slightly in this holistic teaching fold, Cindy brings all of these differences to bear.

Cindy: *I agree with you to a certain extent, Dorothy. Student achievement is an important purpose of education, but when we talk about student achievement, we are talking about learning. For a lot of experts and researchers, doing well on standardized tests and developing deep understanding of subject content are not mutually exclusive. In fact, that is why I think it's important that we should unpack our state learning standards like Grant Wiggins and Jay McTighe suggest in "Understanding by Design [UbD]." I think a crucial step is to specify what sort of understanding we are trying to foster in our instruction. They have six facets of understanding that are really similar to Bloom's taxonomy.*

Too often our learning objectives are too vague. What are we expecting our students to do? Do we just want them to recall and explain some facts, interpret the meaning of a text, apply key concepts to a real life situation? It is really important to move past regurgitating information. We want to be intentional about promoting higher order thinking.

As they say, "begin with the end in mind." What do we want students to know, understand, and be able to do? Once we know that, it's a matter of selecting the most appropriate combination of instructional strategies for delivering the curriculum. The end we want should be the driving force for teachers' teaching and students' learning.

Jim: *UbD certainly does offer us important nuances in terms of the nature of human understanding, Cindy. But to what degree might UbD be limiting? Might it be at times misleading or reinforcing a fixed structure for understanding? You see, Wiggins and McTighe are still locked into Tyler's reductionist logic and technical rationality. Subject matter understanding is a good step, but what about the democratic self and social understandings? What about the existential journeying and inspired leading? Is there not more to being an educator than being a content expert? Holistic pedagogical artistry, contrastively, might offer us a much less restrained endeavor than adhering to prescribed instructional strategies or even scripted techniques.*

Cindy: *Well that is what I like about UbD, it is important to be intentional and the facets of understanding that require the greatest challenge are perspective taking, empathy, and self-knowledge. Is that what you are asking about with the self and social understanding?*

Dan: *That is part of it, but the technical rationality removes the value judgment from the deliberation. By "beginning with the end in mind," the teacher predetermines what constitutes empathy and even "self-knowledge."*

Jen: *I'd add that beginning with the end in mind has always felt for me too much like a unidirectional transmission of knowledge from teacher to student.*

Add to the mix the value neutrality you're pointing to, Dan. It's also a problem. Values pervade everything we do, even if we are not aware of them. Everyone has a perspective. How do values become embodied? The point is for teachers to facilitate as well as embody open-minded and open-hearted reflective inquiries and deliberative conversations in the hopes of creating space for students to cultivate their holistic understandings.

Dorothy: *Okay everyone, I really think we need to be careful with all of that. Schools have a lot of people, and you cannot have too many cooks in the kitchen when you want to get things done and keep things moving forward smoothly. We have to keep everything moving forward in our schools. From a principal's perspective, I don't know if I want teachers all across the building thinking that it is up to them to decide what to teach, when they should teach it, and how. In many cases, a district has curriculum specialists, who have been working really hard on these things. As a principal, I want to know what we have to do, before I start a big conversation about what we want to do or what we value. Besides, a big conversation like the one you're talking about would be incredibly time consuming. Not to mention being a logistical nightmare. You know, as well as I do, the school days are incredibly jam packed with so much to do already. Part of this is I'm just trying to protect teachers' time too as well as leaders.*

Dan: *While I'm listening to you both, there seems to be a key dilemma. Cindy is deferring practical judgments to the intellectual authority of particular educational scholars, researchers, or professional organizations, while Dorothy, you're deferring to institutional authorities within the district and state levels.*

Cindy: *I like your point, Dan, and that's right. I want my doctors to make decisions based on current medical research. So, why wouldn't we want the same in the case of our schools? I want my kids' teachers to make decisions based on the most current consensus derived from educational research, in particular the research coming from their content areas. If a school isn't up to speed with the consensus research-based best practices of leading professional organizations, I wouldn't want them educating my kid. Just like, I wouldn't take anyone in my family to a hospital that conducts blood-lettings as a cure cancer for example.*

Dorothy: *To your comments, Cindy that is the reason I said what I did. Maybe I am deferring to institutional authorities, but I do so to keep "blood-lettings" from happening. Hospitals have regulations and so should schools. The people on top know what the professional organizations say are best practices, and we have come a long way developing systems for making sure good teaching filters down into every classroom. When I was a teacher, my principal never stepped foot in my classroom. No one, except me, has any idea what I was doing. Now, the state mandates a process for evaluating teacher effectiveness and quality teaching is no longer a matter of one person's opinion. With this new mandate, there is a rubric for principals to use when they go into classrooms. This tool can help them see where teachers are performing well and where they are not.*

Then, based on the evaluations teachers and data from the rubrics teaches can adjust their teaching accordingly.

Cindy: *I think that can support the implementation of best practices, but there is more to it than that. It is just a framework, not a strategy.*

Dorothy: *The whole evaluation system the state has though is based on the Danielson framework. It is all in there: planning, classroom environment, instruction, and professionalism. The same rubric is also used for National Board Certification. We have our specialists who are choosing programs and developing pacing guides. We have a rubric that clearly defines what good teachers do, and we have testing structures in place to make sure students are learning. Why do we need to go about trying to reinvent the wheel? Trust me, this is enough to keep us busy! And enough to address in our educational leadership program here at the college.*

Jim: *Some important pedagogical questions come to my mind as we're talking here. How might we engage in a broader dialogue about what constitutes pedagogical excellence? How might we disrupt the dominant discourse of effective teaching, which is often taken for granted? How might we demonstrate the constructive, pragmatic implications of classrooms as site for creative democracy?*

Dan: *Sometimes I would make decisions in my classroom not knowing what would come of it. A small group might create a mural together. Or, I would come across a favorite folk tale in the library and stop everything, so we could all sit down and enjoy a magnificent story. One time, I learned of a very shy student's fascination with turtles. The next day, I brought in books, an art project, and a short movie about turtles. We had a day that was all about turtles. Also, there were days when the season was changing and we just went outside for a walk and a chance to observe nature and each other. Of course, every now and then, I would become worried that life was getting too serious in kindergarten; so, I would randomly turn on disco music signaling to the children that it was time to take a break, dance, and be silly. I had no predetermined learning objectives, and fortunately, these activities were not subjected the scrutiny of Danielson's rubric. However, when teenagers and young college students contact me to reminisce about kindergarten memories, these are the sorts of things they want to talk about. These are the experiences that seemed to have enduring value.*

Jen: *I really appreciate your questions, Jim and what you're sharing with us, Dan. It's important. The educational experiences you're recalling are expressions of sensitivity, freedom, caring, creativity, and intelligence in your practice as a pedagogical artist. Clearly, such experiences were rich with holistic meanings for you, as the teacher, and for your students. You were making in-action qualitative judgments; you were attentive to open ends; you were not seeking control. Your thoughts triggered my memories of building a wigwam in 3rd grade with our student teacher. For weeks, he trekked outside with twenty or so* *eight- or nine-year-olds, and together we got our hands dirty gathering thatch, bark, and sticks tied them into bundles, bent branches, and fastened pieces to a wooden frame.*

Occasionally, I drive by my elementary school and look at the spot where we built it, which is no longer a forest of pines but a parking lot for a Hilton Garden Inn. Our student teacher probably had some objectives or standards tied to what we were doing, or maybe not. Who knows, I was a kid then. I think the whole of that experience was the value not marking off a standard. The learning to problem solve together and the feelings of excitement, wonder, failure, determination, cooperate, and accomplishment had enduring value—at least for me. It would be interesting to know what my classmates might recall from then too.

UNPACKING THE COLLEGIAL EXCHANGE

Like in the prior chapter, here we pause to consider distinctions between the pedagogical approaches advanced by Dorothy and Cindy alongside our conceptual platform. Dorothy and Cindy both show tendencies to perceive curriculum as an artifact, object, credential, program, and/or training procedure. For them, curriculum is a sort of *thing* that is external from us. Curriculum is something we are given. It is what we look to for what to do. Part of what holistic teaching does is challenge us to think about is the notion that curriculum is not solely as an observable object external from you and your students. Holistic teaching also positions curriculum as transactional; it is alive, dynamic. Curriculum exists in spaces where minds, bodies, hearts, guts, souls, memories, values, histories, relationships, and more collide. Dorothy and Cindy do, however, demonstrate two tacit ways curriculum is commonly taken up. Dorothy has an inclination to rule over subordinate practitioners and acquiesce to those in positions of greater authority. Cindy seems more interested in leveraging intellectual authority and being the advice-giving experts.

Deferring to institutionalized authorities, Dorothy made reference to the Danielson Framework. Charlotte Danielson (2007) developed a rubric for evaluating teacher effectiveness, which Dorothy correctly points out has been mandated by her state's Department of Education. Dorothy applauds the efficiency of the rubric. She finds its ready-made, behavioral criteria helpful for principals, who want to complete teacher evaluations without getting lost in the complexities and ambiguities of debating what constitutes good teaching. Aligned with the purposes she articulated, the rubric maintains an orderly sense of consistency from classroom to classroom, across a build, districts, and even a whole state or states.

On the other hand, Cindy expressed less affinity for the Danielson rubrics. However, her tempered enthusiasm stops short of an engaging in robust critique. Reminding us, "it is just a framework, not a strategy," provides only a first step toward the pedagogical artistry we have in mind with the holistic teaching fold. Cindy is not at all bothered by the instrumentalist focus of the teacher evaluation rubrics. The rubric does not conflict with her commitments to curriculum design or thorough approach to craft reflection. In fact, Cindy's presumptions that learning goals as well as instructional methods are uniform, not contextual bound, and can be predetermined are supported by the state mandated rubric. Further, the notion that all educational experiences are comprised of teachers functioning as knowledge producers and students acquiring new knowledge is reinforcement by Cindy's endeavor to bridge theory and practice.

Having acquired the knowledge through academic study, Cindy considers herself uniquely positioned on a metaphorical assembly line. By reproducing knowledge from the academy among K-12 colleagues, she presumably bolsters the productivity of theory and research, while also augmenting teachers' efficiency and effectiveness as knowledge producers. All this in turn benefits students in acquiring content knowledge. Though Dorothy might see the criteria on state sanctioned teacher effectiveness rubric as ends in themselves and conducive to improving test scores, Cindy considers the rubric as a potentially helpful scaffolding for supporting deeper subject matter learning.

With our vision for holistic teaching, we have more transactional view of educational experience in mind. From our perspective, teacher effectiveness rubrics are counter-productive for fostering pedagogical artistry. Beginning with the foundations of the most commonly appropriated rubric, Danielson advances an ahistorical, decontextualized, impersonal rendering of educational science to discredit a superficial view of pedagogical artistry. Crediting Madelyn Hunter's work in the 1970s and 1980s as being the originator of a science of teaching, Danielson (2007) erroneously suggests, "Hunter was one of the first educators to argue persuasively that teaching is not only an art but also a science" (p. 7). Overlooking the contrasting views of educational science put forth by Dewey and Thorndike in the early 1900s, Danielson propagates a Thorndikian view of teaching, characterized by direct instruction, as though it were an innovative idea.

Elliot Eisner (1994) is important here because he pointed out how Thorndike's view of educational science carried the day in the industrial era, because scientific management more neatly coincided with social efficiency movement and factory model schooling. In this sense, Danielson's framework is an edict of a century-long heritage of appealing to bureaucratic penchant for upholding authoritative hierarchies. However, the range of ideas that can function within the Danielson framework (represented here by Dorothy's and Cindy's comments), should not overshadow the restrictions placed on teachers' experimentation and imagination. Following Eisner, we hope to revitalize a Deweyan heritage recognizing teaching as the supreme art in a society with democratic aspirations.

Teachers and students alike are on parallel, idiosyncratic journeys of understanding. If a teacher's experience is guided by deferring to a hierarchy of authority, than there is a strong likelihood that students will be encouraged to demonstrate similar deference. However, if teachers embrace existential journey of holistic 3S understanding, they are likewise positioned to facilitate their students' 3S journeys. It is worth reiterating key attributes for what it is we mean by pedagogical artistry.

Our conjecture is that dedicated educators—acting with a sense of vocational calling—do not function as detached technicians or objective scientists in a laboratory. They feel a discord with such a vision of being an educator. Holistic teaching has a very different felt quality to it in that it acknowledges educators make tacit judgments throughout the course of a school day. Stop and think for a moment about all the judgements you make during a day of teaching. If you are not presently in a classroom, imagine it. These judgments are based on commitments to inclusive, caring relationships and not a cold analysis of data collected by standardized measures. Teachers possess potentially irreplaceable insights into problem solving and sometimes in the real-time of classrooms they follow their instincts. Based on relationships that can only be fostered through their close proximity to students, creative teachers, often to the chagrin of Charlotte Danielson (2007), embrace the emergence of what Elliot Eisner called expressive outcomes.

In our conversation about facilitating educational experiences, Dorothy and Cindy acted in a manner consistent with the clearly stated learning objectives they advanced in the previous chapter 3. Approaching teaching-learning as a task of transferring fixed knowledge from teacher to student, they again exclusively attend to the technical strategies of teaching. Of course, Cindy deepens the technical enterprise by considering teaching not only for knowledge retention but also for subject-matter understanding. Conversely, we (Jim, Jen, and Dan) are attempting to invite a conversation about holistic, transactional pedagogy. Our attempts to advance pedagogical artistry is also aligned with the aims talking demonstrated in the previous chapter on educational purposes. Here we are advancing pedagogical practices that encourages having "power-with" students and students' cultivating their "power from within," which is consistent with Dewey's vision of teachers functioning as supreme artists of a society with democratic aspirations.

PARTING THOUGHTS

Envisioning the transactional artistry at the heart of holistic teaching might still be challenging. Holistic teaching might even feel uncomfortable at times. Know that all this is okay. It can be challenging to picture and feel what something is especially if we do not have much firsthand, lived experience with it. Part of the challenge of holistic teaching is that we find ourselves in a dominant culture that promotes us to continuously focuses our attention toward standardized teaching and learning. This is highly problematic, because when our time, energies, and attention continuously focus on something like "getting everyone on the same page," that becomes what we will continue to see and move forward doing. But there is always so much more happening than what we end up focusing on. Holistic teaching honors and explores all the "stuff" that standardization overlooks. Holistic teaching pushes us to work in generative ways because there are no step-by-step guides or set of directions to tell us how to do it. After all, transactional artistry has no predetermined beginnings and no ends rather is about gaining more and more experience with problem solving that advances democratic values in our classrooms.

In this chapter, we advance a vision of holistic teaching. Holistic teaching is about being mindful and having deliberations about the tone and conditions of our classrooms and schools. The dominant educational culture explicitly and implicitly reinforces certain conditions. Holistic teaching, however, is about fostering and empowering students' democratic learning as well as embracing intellectual, emotional, and spiritual growth. When educators are committed to cultivating their holistic, democratic journeys of understanding, they can be models for students. Appreciating that holistic teaching works against the grain of the organizational structures prevailing in American schools, the next fold, that is generative lead-learning, will focus on how we might organize ourselves to cultivate the practice of 3S pedagogical artistry.

Pause and Ponder

As we did in the professional awakening fold, we end this fold with a set of questions that can aid you in beginning to take stock of how things are going within the holistic teaching fold.

- How am I doing with creating spaces for encouraging and fostering my *students' holistic journeys of 3S understanding*?
- How am I doing with fostering a *democratic space* in my classroom with my students?
- In what sense am I learning from my students as part of my experience teaching them?
- How am I making sense of my *past, present,* and *future* in ways that encourage expressing and infusing holistic teaching into my classroom?
- How might I persisting in being *open-mind* and *open-hearted* when the norms and circumstances I find myself in feel and are otherwise?

DELVING DEEPER: STUDY RESOURCES

Below we leave a set of offerings that have informed our thinking on the holistic teaching fold. Again, these resources may not directly use the label of holistic teaching, but we have found their contents thought-provoking in various ways. As you keep reading, we highly encourage you to find connects to resources you have encountered that you feel resonate with holistic teaching and the other folds in this book.

Miller, J. P. (2006). *Educating for wisdom and compassion: Creating conditions for timeless learning.* Thousand Oaks, CA: Corwin Press.
Miller, J. P. (2007). *The holistic curriculum.* Toronto, Canada: University of Toronto Press.
   Both of John Miller's books are stellar resources when it comes to contemplating the nature of holistic education. He challenges dualistic educational thought, acknowledges the interdependence of all life, and works toward a wisdom-seeking consciousness.

Garrison, J. (1997). *Dewey and Eros: Wisdom and Desire in the Art of Teaching.* New York, NY: Teachers College Press.

Jim Garrison's book will offer you a strong interpretation and application of John Dewey's philosophical thoughts in relationship to education. In the book, Garrison invites us to question what is of value in education, why it is we teach, and what it means to learn.

hooks, b. (1994). *Teaching to transgress: Education as the practice of freedom*. New York, NY: Routledge.
A classic with respects to critically examining social structures that govern our cultural and individual landscapes, bell hooks encourages us to explore how education, learning, and teaching can create open, democratic spaces rather than directorial, oppressive ones. She stresses the need for educators to have an awareness of the mind/body/spirit connection inherent to our inner well-being and journeys of self-actualization.

Buzzelli, C., & Johnston, B. (2002). *The moral dimensions of teaching: Language, power, and culture in classroom interactions*. New York, NY: RoutledgeFalmer.
This book provides a rich description of aspects of classroom life that too often get overlooked in research and practice. The way teachers engage with discourse, authority, and diverse identities is thoughtfully analyzed in this book.

Ryan, F. X. (2011). *Seeing together: Mind, matter and the experimental outlook of John Dewey and Arthur F. Bentley*. Great Barrington, MA: American Institute for Economic Research.
Frank Ryan is an academic philosopher with extensive expertise in John Dewey's expansive body of scholarship. In this book, Ryan provides a nuanced explanation of some of Dewey's most impenetrable writings in an accessible manner. Dewey's late career shifts toward a transactional perspective are explained in this book.

REFERENCES

Blumenfeld-Jones, D. S. (2012). *Curriculum and the aesthetic life: Hermeneutics, body, democracy and ethics in curriculum theory and practice*. New York, NY: Peter Lang.

Danielson, C. (2007). *Enhancing professional practice: A framework for teaching* (2nd ed.). Alexandria, VA: Association for Supervision and Curriculum Development.

Eisner, E. W. (1994). *The educational imagination: On the design and evaluation of school programs* (3rd ed.). New York, NY: Macmillan.

Schubert, W. H. (2010). Curriculum studies, definitions and dimensions of. In C. Kridel (Ed.), *Encyclopedia of curriculum studies* (Vol. 1, pp. 230–38). Los Angeles, CA: Sage Publications.

Chapter Four

Generative Lead-Learning

How are we reorganizing for an authentic culture that nurtures the capacity building that this pedagogical artistry requires?

Throughout this book, we have been contrasting competing paradigms in an attempt to illustrate that so many of our educational institutions are not organized toward awakening and cultivating educators' artistry. Indeed, existential journeys and democratic collegiality are often stultified by a dominant paradigm, characterized by credentialing criteria for becoming a "master teacher," notions of best practices, and accountability systems. In this climate, teachers are urged to know, that is, to efficiently instruct and demonstrate their effectiveness in having students attain standardized outcomes. From a wisdom-seeking paradigm, however, we are encouraging educators to reflect, deliberate, and inquire as lead-learners aspiring toward evolving, indeterminate aims. Within this chapter we will continue to explore such ideas with reference to how we might begin to reorganize ourselves in ways that nurture educators' generative lead-learning.

Reorganizing ourselves in schools to function in a democratic fashion, instead of the typical top-down organizational structure of schools, constitutes at least three important criteria. First, an authentic culture welcomes the participation of diverse and sometimes competing ideas and interests. The authentic participation of diverse stakeholders provides the substance of how democracy works. Second, participants in an authentic culture strive to function in a generative manner. As curriculum leader expresses their points of view in an authentic culture, they do so in a way that invites dialogue and a willingness to respectfully listen to stakeholders with contrasting and even opposing viewpoints. While curriculum leaders may offer an idea and perhaps a persuasive argument to be considered among the other stakeholders, they are not looking to shut down opposing points of view. Third, the authentic and generative qualities are further refined by leaders' positioning themselves as learners. Thus, inviting and embodying inquiry is the best way to personify generative lead-learning.

Within the dominant paradigm teachers have grown accustomed to various discourses of professional development. Following an essentialist philosophy of education, teacher competency is often assessed in reference to a static set of knowledge, skills, and dispositional qualities. For example, teachers' alleged competency can easily be assessed by testing their knowledge of recognized "best practices" or content knowledge. Lee Schulman's (1986) work developed this aspect of professional competency even further with his conceptualization of pedagogical content knowledge. Pedagogical content knowledge is a professional competency that combines what a teacher knows about the curricular content for which she/he is responsible and what she/he knows about instructional strategies. Although common sense calls for teachers to know both their content and how to teach, Shulman's important fusing of these bases of knowledge is often overlooked within the habituated organizational structures of most schools.

Instructional effectiveness rubrics provide a uniform tool for assessing skill and dispositional compliance is often maintained under the guise of professionalism. Moreover, such rubrics are applied uniformly to teachers regardless of what grade level or subject matter they teach. The criteria for state teacher evaluation systems, master teacher credentials, or National Board Certification are generally uniform and have not changed much since their time of conception. For instance, see Charlotte Danielson's (2007) *Enhancing Professional Practice: A Framework for Teaching* to see the image of the skilled professional that is being circulated, albeit occasionally retitled, by the various powers that be. Dispositionally, the dominant paradigm values compliance and conformity. With rhetoric of innovation and teacher leadership, hierarchies of authority are maintained. Administrators are deemed the "gates keepers of culture," reinforcing deeply established traditions of subordinating teachers and rendering phrases like "teacher leadership" oxymoronic, because a teacher will never in actuality been positioned as someone with equal authority to a school leader.

In order to illustrate the habituated bureaucratic hierarchies of schools' organizational structure, we call your attention to the image below. Experienced educators are surely aware of and have encountered structures of top-down management illustrated in the figure. An ordinary organizational hierarchy chart can easily capture how the typical chain of command is followed beginning with the a state department administration. Located in the image are families and communities, but they remain at a distance. Their peripheral

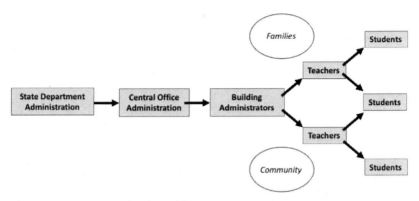

Figure 4.1. Bureaucratic Hierarchies

location is because they are one degree removed from the bureaucratic hierarchy and flow of accountability within schooling. Families and communities are generally speaking not overly important to the technical procedures used for control in educational systems.

As alluded to in previous folds, the complex, intellectually demanding, and inherently ethical enterprise of teaching is too often appraised from a reductionist, decontextualized, impersonal, and disembodied frame of reference. What might change if we looked to extraordinary teachers as exemplars instead of the presumptions embedded in established structures and traditions? What if persons like Confucius, Socrates, Mother Teresa, John Dewey, Eleanor Roosevelt, Mahatma Gandhi, Martin Luther King, Jr., the Dalai Lama, and others were inspirational models for our professional lives? Would the value of institutional habits be put in proper perspective? Most importantly, how might we function differently, as educational professionals?

A GENERATIVE LEAD-LEARNING PORTRAIT

Generative lead-learning, as we are envisioning it, embraces uncertainty. Moreover, in different ways and in different contexts, the exemplars mentioned above also embrace diverse perspectives and even disagreement. In order to avoid the pretense of idealism, however, it is greatly important to recognize that our schools are not set up in such a way, nor have they ever really been. Generative lead-learning runs against the grain of centuries of institutional habits in the American school system. Further, recalling that Socrates was sentenced to death by hemlock for his impiety and corrupting minds, it is not inaccurate to assert that in some ways generative lead-learning also goes against the grain of the deeper structures of millenniums of Western heritage. It is perhaps even a deep challenge to the evolution of our human consciousnesses? The great teachers, mentioned above, spoke truth to power in meaningful ways often discouraged by dominant culture. Therefore, democratically inspired educators face challenges that are as old as the practice of teaching itself. We must contend with the ethical and aesthetic sterility of standardized-management consciousness creates empty rhetoric and sloganeering that is pernicious. Doublespeak abounds in schools, and such discourse wants us to coexist unproblematically with contradictory practices. To live an examined life and to walk the talk of democratic values in schools is undoubtedly as challenging as it is fulfilling.

The predominance of management culture organizes educational stakeholders within hierarchical systems, assigning clearly defined roles and responsibilities to each individual. Additionally, top-down management encourages one to look up the ladder of authority to find ready answers, paving a path of least resistance. However, generative lead-learning embodies

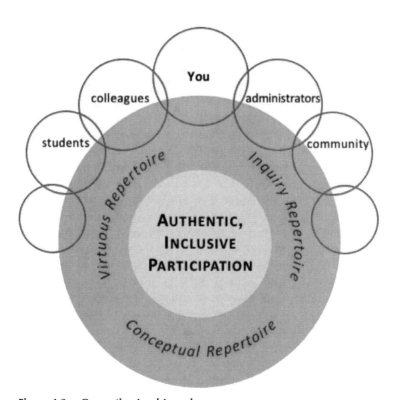

Figure 4.2.   Generative Lead-Learning

a "power from within" and "power-with" orientation to educational institutions. We, again, have generated a visual in an attempt to capture a feel for what generative lead-learning might look like, an image of interconnectedness and coming together. The figure above is our attempt to capture a sense of the relational nature of generative lead-learning.

Generative lead-learning contrasts management culture's desires for control and "power-over" people. Instead of looking upward to an authority figure to clarify professional or student learning outcomes, we envision professional educators, administrators, students, community members, and other educational stakeholders working cooperatively toward building and refining their conceptual, reflective, and virtuous repertoires. We touch upon these repertoires in more details later in this chapter. At the heart of generative lead-learning is seeking to cultivate authentic, inclusive participation from many. Most schools think about, discuss, and enact professionalism value-neutral terms and structures. Re-organizing ourselves as generative lead-learners is a visionary and democratic aspiration informed by sustained reflective inquiry enriched by deliberative conversation.

In school improvement efforts, educators routinely attach great importance to collaboration, an example of this can be seen in Professional Learning Communities (PLCs). While collaboration and structures, such as PLCs, can obviously support educators' technical decision-making, they do so separately from the implicit and less frequently discussed value judgments, which are embedded in all educational courses of action. As with the other folds, generative lead-learning does not separate fact and values. Therefore, we propose the technical reflection that routinely and collaboratively occurs in PLCs ought to be expanded to include various forms of reflective inquiries. Educators ought to reflectively inquire into the not only technical but also the dynamic complexities of their daily practices that are always all at once personal, critical, ethical, and political.

Often with extreme zeal for specificity, the collaborative processes in PLCs stifle educators' professional learning. Emphasizing consistency among teachers, PLCs often uphold an image of professionalism based on sanctioned credentials and observable competencies. In a sense, professional development mirrors the knowledge transmission approach to teaching and learning discussed in the previous chapter. Generative lead-learning encompasses these particular professional learning experiences within more expansive aims of cultivating democratic virtues. Wanting teachers to function as free-thinking lead professionals, generative lead-learning involves an ongoing journey of disciplined study and practice to develop conceptual, reflective inquiry, and virtuous repertoires. In contrast to knowledge transmission, this form of professional learning exemplifies a transactional quality that connects educational activities, aims of understanding, and living democratically good lives.

Generative lead-learning is not only a cultural challenge but also an individual developmental issue. With these in mind, this fold attends to presuppositions about the ways in which human beings grow and learn, or what is often called developmental theory. In chapter 1, we referenced Martha Nussbaum's (2011) capabilities approach to understanding human development. A capabilities approach to development recognizes the dynamic relationship between an individual's agency and socio-cultural circumstances. Being or becoming a capable educator is not simply about allowing innate capacities, such as intelligence, natural talents, or other abilities, to unfold. Additionally, being or becoming a capable educator cannot be sufficiently understood as a process of being conditioned by ideal environmental factors. Democracy as a moral standard of living is yet to be fully realized anywhere in the globe, although some places and persons are more full-bodied expressions of it than others. Therefore, supposing that any educational leaders can shepherd their colleagues out of incompetent darkness and into the light of competency is a stance of profound self-righteous arrogance. No one individual nor any group of individuals is the savior or liberator with all the perfect answers to our educational problems. Being generative encourages us to be sensitive toward others as well as attentive to the ongoing growth and learning we and others undergo.

From a more transactional viewpoint, an individual's interests, aspirations, and abilities are inseparable from the contextualizing social, economic, and political conditions. The dominant discourse organizes curriculum—correspondingly teachers' and students' experiences—from unwarranted positions of certainty, explicitly clarified by learning objectives. In far too many school settings, uncertainty is a sign of incompetence, and disagreement is perceived as toxicity and something to be dodge. When it is ethically and politically sterile, dominant educational discourse demands demonstrations of developmental and cultural norms, which are specifically predetermined competency behaviors and consensus-driven collaboration. For example, frameworks for teacher effectiveness alleged essential "professional competencies" but oversimplify the complexities of teaching. PLCs allegedly support dialogue and collaboration among colleagues, however, presumptuously insisting on consensus building and at times may get caught up with inauthentic initiative. This can especially be the case when a readily agreed on answer is not there. Demands for conformity stifle teachers' professional agency and an authentic, democratic cultural support.

Fundamentally, generative lead-learning focuses on how we might go about organizing ourselves to promote pluralism and holistic human flourishing through educational experiences with each other. Experienced educators will recognize that the dominant paradigm offers an abundant supply of ready-made answers. Experienced educators are also probably very familiar with the top-down management structures that pervade education institutions in the United States. Of course, professional competency is preferable to abject incompetence; it is highly unlikely that you have met an educator who did not want to be "effective." But, we ask: What constitutes teacher effectiveness? For years, educational scholars and practitioners have been lamenting the isolation of teachers. Advocating for collaborations through things like PLCs is nothing new, and finding an educational leader who does not set out to "support" colleagues is probably as futile as an effort to locate a deliberately incompetent teacher.

Generative lead-learning is interdependent of the other folds. Part of professional awakening is to feel and understand the effect of educational doublespeak, enliven a sense of artistry, and cultivate critical consciousness. Far too often educators uncritically accept vacuous terms (e.g., competency, effectiveness, collaboration, and support) to organize their professional endeavors. Worse, not only does such educational discourse obscure the deeper aims or aspirations of educational enterprise, but the implied meaning of vacuous terms is often reversed when concretized into research, policy, and practice. Within the dominant discourse competence becomes compliance; effectiveness is equated to predictableness; collaboration means conformity; support plays out in the form of management. With all this in mind, perhaps the first step of advancing personal and generative leadership is to distinguish holistic journeys of understanding inspired by a love of wisdom from euphemisms hiding a management agenda.

The well-known public intellectual and curriculum and pedagogy scholar, Nel Noddings (2013) points us toward the importance of educational aims. She succinctly explains, "we point to aims when we are asked, or ask ourselves, why we are engaged in certain activities and why we are committed to certain beliefs and practices" (p. 40). Aims talking is a more expansive conversation than specifying educational goals or objectives for professionals or for children. Generative lead-learning takes Noddings's broader view to heart with organizing curriculum, with attention to interdisciplinary breadth and humanistic depth, in contrast to bureaucratic systems of instructional management.

How do human beings learn, grow, and develop? How might professional educators organize themselves to nurture authentic human flourishing that balances individual moral agency and collegial social responsibility? If educators are to function as "dynamic creators of meaning" (Joseph, 2000), they must be able to engage in professional contexts with a sense of personal agency. Generative collaborations are characterized by your ideas, beliefs, feelings, as well as the opportunity to freely articulate your perspective and participate in substantial decisions and value judgments. Educational professionals are not interchangeable widgets of machine. Schools, and all the begins within them, are better understood as dynamically, evolving ecologies than static socializing mechanisms. When we attend to the inherent moral and political dimensions of teaching, substantive individual freedoms are balanced with social responsibilities that change and transform cultural conditions.

A DELIBERATIVE CONVERSATION

Now, let us re-enter our ongoing dialogue with Dorothy and Cindy. Our common ground with Dorothy and Cindy around Tyler's rationale might be an entry point for collegial dialogue, and maybe potentially for engaging in generative lead-learning. That said, however, perhaps the greatest disparity between our two colleagues' platforms and ours is the degree to which we seek to embrace and encourage deliberating and negotiating education with reference to the complexities and ambiguities of democratic living. Both Dorothy and Cindy, to a lesser degree, possess understandings that teaching, curriculum, and leadership as separate activities with clearly defined boundaries and trajectories. Put another way, there are certain organizational structures at play and a minimal desire to challenge or re-imagine them.

Take as an example how Dorothy and Cindy accept the dominant discourse and reinforce habits that efficient productivity is a hallmark of "good" schools and that there are distinct jobs for those who do curriculum, teaching, and leading. Teachers' productivity is measured by the productivity of their students; meanwhile, the educational leaders' chief purpose is to increase productivity by having keep things in the school running smoothly. Leaders are responsible for keeping the efficient school machine well-oiled and on time with maximum output within budget. Our discussion now begins to shift focus toward considering how we might organize, or structure, our educational problem solving. The conversation begins with Dorothy responding to Dan's and Jen's ending comments in the holistic teaching fold. Dan was reflecting on his experiences with his kindergarteners; meanwhile, Jen recalled an experience from third grade.

> **Dorothy** (beginning with a jestful tone): *Where was your principal, Dan when you were taking all of those breaks, goofing around? But, seriously . . . I'm not against having fun every once in while in schools or at recesses, but there is serious work to be done in kindergarten. In all honesty, if I were your principal I wouldn't stop the good times, as long as they didn't get excessive. But, I would let you know that it was noticed, and I would make it clear that I better not see those little kiddos in your class next year not ready for first grade.*

Cindy: *As an instructional coach, I have to interject. There are wonderful ways that the activities Dan described could be thoughtfully done. Taking a nature walk, doing art projects, certainly reading folk tales are all excellent learning activities. My questions would be: How are you incorporating standards? What did you want students to know, understand, and be able to do as a result of those activities?*

Jen: *But aren't some activities worth doing, even if they don't have some sort of practical purpose? Aren't some experiences worth having even if you don't know the end result beforehand? I think about when I'm creating artworks for example. They're not always tethered to a practical pre-determined purpose and the vast majority of the time I could have never known beforehand what I would have generated by the end. In fact, some pieces don't even reach an "end" and others get disregarded because they don't work, feel right, or my interest wanes.*

Other examples come to my mind too. We might experience a concert, a book, a sporting event, a national monument, a winery, a forest, or a movie without knowing what thoughts or feelings will be evoked. Even with the places we go to every day, like schools or grocery stores, we do not always know what we will feel or what will happen. I can pass a person on the street but what will happen in the next twelve steps, I have no idea. At times, generating understandings about ourselves and others is about embracing the unknown and unpredictable elements of the experience. Experiences can be worth having even if we can't see results. Sometimes we need to let go of our inner desires for control.

Cindy: *But, as a classroom teacher, isn't it his job to connect experiences to standards? Those are great things to do, and I'm all for extra-curricular activities. But I don't know if a teacher is doing their job if they can't say how an activity is building on prior knowledge and leading into future learning.*

Dan: *Does it matter if the learning standards are identified prior to the experience though? Learning happened during these activities, but often in ways that I didn't anticipate. Learning is also about time too. At times we can have experiences but connects might not happen right away. Is it really essential for a teacher to predict and control the outcomes of every educational experience?*

Dorothy: *Somethings are really simple. There is a clear trajectory, defining students' progress. That is why we are so concerned about keeping everyone "on grade level." This is why we have curriculum maps, programs, and pacing guides that are connected to the standards. They come from the district level. Like I told you before, if you start getting too creative or philosophical about things you are going to get yourself in trouble. For all practical purposes, it all starts with the standards. I want all of the standards to be covered and assessed. Since the teacher is in control of classroom activities, I think that they should be held accountable for connecting instruction to the standards. I think this is something that can be controlled. There has to be structure!*

Cindy: *From my perspective, PLCs are powerful for that kind of accountability.*
If a teacher is starting to get carried away with activities-based lesson planning,
their PLC can remind them to think about the standards being covered. That is
why the UbD lesson and unit planning templates are so valuable. They keep us
intentional with our instruction. By beginning with the end in mind, the assess-
ment, teachers have to account up front for what students will know, understand
and be able to do.

UNPACKING THE COLLEGIAL EXCHANGE

Our present fold focuses on the organizational structures that scaffold our
daily lives in schools and the educational problem solving that unfolds around
and within them. Expressions of different views of how to plan and carry out
educational experiences are vividly contrasted in the conversation you just
read. You will likely notice—as did Ralph Tyler—that matters of purpose are
intimately related to the experiences that educators will envision and enact.
Dorothy's and Cindy's external locus of control and divisions between teaching, leadership, and curriculum restricts their pedagogical imaginations in an
important way. As was the case in previously folds, Dorothy's approach feels
a bit more rigid than Cindy's. What is particularly interesting, however, is their
shared understanding of what it means to be practical. For them, being practical is organized around ways one is expected to exercise power and control
within bureaucratic structures. Leaders are at the top of the food chain and
exert "power over" teachers. The leaders can be administrators in the school
and/or governmental-based departments of education. Meanwhile, teachers
are in control students. Students are supposed to be in control of their learning.

To be practical, according to Tyler, is to engage in an ongoing process of
technical reflection and problem solving. Again emphasizing here the organizational structures that guide one's problem-solving process, Dorothy correctly argues that schools and classrooms need to have structure. If not, they
may run the risk of devolving into a state of chaos. Structures of institutional
authority, however, narrow her problem-solving process. In fact, aligning
with the desires of her supervisor seems to define her narrowly conceptualized purposes, which lead to dutiful courses of action, exhibiting a diligent
sense of compliance. Considering multiple perspectives, or even developing
her own, is sadly deemed a waste of time within Dorothy's atheoretical commitment to practice.

Cindy, on the other hand, does seem to have a more individualized sense of
professional purpose. Yet, for her, fixed notions of best practices structure her
problem solving in a way that is almost as unwavering as Dorothy's form of
rigidity. Cindy's appraisal of pedagogical quality is with reference to the au-

thoritative consensus of particular professional organizations. Though Cindy may not be as rigid as Dorothy in her deference to school authorities, Cindy's interest in divergent viewpoints is inspired only within the boundaries of pre-conceived ideas about *good* teaching. Thus, Cindy also strictly adheres to a source of authority, albeit a different source than Dorothy.

A second issue exists with the dominant approach to curriculum and in-structional problem solving demonstrated by Dorothy and Cindy. In two different ways, our hypothetical colleagues decontextualized their perspectives. Deferring all judgment to the norms expressed by institutional authorities. For Dorothy, leadership overlooks the dynamic variations from classroom to classroom. While Cindy's reverence to instructional best practices, also fail to consider context with any degree of depth. Instead of accounting for the milieu of a particular place, for example a community, school, or classroom, Cindy is committed to generalizing the consensus guidelines for instructional to all classroom. Again, in two distinctive ways, Dorothy and Cindy propa-gate a standardized-management consciousness through their unexamined adherence to established organizational structures. Where is their inquiry and deep respect for the complexities of educational practice? How might we encourage them to liberate themselves from the recursive cycle of being managed and managing others?

Perhaps, Dorothy's and Cindy's fondness for the established norms already available to them could be brought into a more expansive frame of reference. Instead of inculcating educators to trust in chains of command, or in the panaceas of best practice framework, represented through popular acronyms such as PLCs, UbD, RtI, UDL (to name just a few), generative lead-learning is about reframing educational problem-solving enterprises as an endeavor of cultivating capabilities. Advancing generative lead-learning is a discipline "from within" that is actualized through our individual existential journey of understanding. From this vantage point, there is no such thing as a "master teacher." We are all on different journeys and in an endless in a state of growth and learning.

Generative lead-learning draws on a balance of skepticism and hope. We are skeptical of readily available and uniform answers, such as "high-impact" or evidence-based practices. Moreover, we are equally skeptical of technical strategies that maintain a sense of ethical or political sterility, such as collabo-rating among "professional learning communities." To be clear, the skepticism we intend to express is not dismissive of the value of these popular educational ideas. We value the contributions of rigorous educational research, derived from multiple theoretical platforms. Additionally, generative lead-learning is also collaborative endeavor. Undoubtedly, technical craft reflection is an im-portant facet of dedicated teachers' efforts to improve their practices. However, generative lead-learning is more multi-faceted, consisting of the development of three repertoires of the course of an educator's career.

In summary, Dorothy and Cindy uncritically accept the traditional hierarchies of authority that often constitute the organizational structures of schools. Through curriculum mapping and bureaucratic protocol educators' roles and responsibilities are clearly defined and assigned. Jim, Jen, and Dan are inviting Dorothy and Cindy to reorganize their professional lives in a way that allows for experimentation with 3S pedagogy in contexts of disciplined academic study, collegial dialogue, and self-examination. In effect, generative lead-learning further advances the democratic values enunciated through aims talking and then transactionally enacted through holistic teaching. Dorothy and Cindy are being invited to consider their potential as intellectual leaders of democratic values, steering their own professional growth, and shaping their own professional culture. The organizational shift from compliance with top-down management to reflective inquiry and deliberative conversation is part of the more expansive effort of trying to realize democratic virtues in educational practices.

CULTIVATING REPERTOIRES

We want to firstly invite you to develop your *conceptual repertoire*. In the preface, introduction, and chapter 1's theoretical platform, we highlighted key concepts that Jim has identified over the course of his career as a curriculum theorist and teacher of curriculum studies. As illustrated by our hypothetical conversation with Dorothy and Cindy, several educators consider theory impractical. Especially since Dorothy and Cindy take pride in being "grounded in practice," they presume conceptual understandings to be impractical. Nothing could be farther from the truth however. Research and practice is always guided by theory, whether it is thoroughly understood or not. Everything we do education—and in life—is informed by a sense of values and of what reality is or is not. Speaking from experience, we can testify that our own efforts to advance curriculum leadership have are often challenged by colleagues who did not appreciate the worth of conceptual clarity. Unfortunately, avoiding theory is never a shortcut for advancing educational problem solving and pedagogical artistry. Ignoring theory is an embrace of unchallenged presuppositions. In this way, Dorothy and Cindy are the norm, not the exception.

Second, we invite you to develop your *reflective repertoire*. This repertoire has two parts. The first is three reflective inquiries that concretize theory in the empirical realities of practice (Henderson et al., 2015). Put differently, these three reflective inquiries are a process for considering how theory (i.e., your conceptual repertoire) meets practice (i.e., your professional journey and your students' personal journeys). Teaching for holistic 3S understanding is a complicated endeavor. Putting theory into practice in his classroom is only half of the story of Jim's experiences working with graduate students at Kent State University. The other half, as was mentioned in chapter 1, is that Jim considered his teaching responsibilities to be action research. In other words, working with graduate students was an opportunity to experiment with ideas and work to refine the nuances of theorizing. Certainly, theory informed and enhanced practice, and visa versa, practice informed and enhanced theorizing.

The next reflective inquiry calls on us to model holistic journeys of understanding. A basic tenet of qualitative inquiry is understanding how the researcher is himself an instrument of analysis. This idea can be extended to educators. One cannot be much help to students' or colleagues' holistic journeys of understanding, if one is not on a wisdom-loving journey oneself. Embodying a love of wisdom is not only a generative process of always learning. It is also a generous process that respects and honors the diverging paths of colleagues on disparate journeys. Amid the frustrations that we might feel during conversations with colleagues who devalue theory or the ethical/political dimensions of education, such as Dorothy and Cindy, we remain committed to modeling the democratic virtues we are trying to advance.

In that spirit we ask you, the reader, to consider alongside us: *How might we invite Dorothy and Cindy into a more conceptually nuanced dialogue in a way that respects their interests and experiences, yet challenges their presuppositions? Would it help to highlight the lack of continuity even between the two of them? How might we do this in ways that are generative and not about finding faults?* Dorothy's steadfast loyalty to district-level administrators and Cindy's assurance in prescriptions derived from leading professional organizations can overlap. However, often times, they often find themselves in conflict. *What do we do when we disagree?* Continuing conversations amid conflicting viewpoints represents a mutually beneficial opportunity to each of us for potential personal development and cultural transformation. Perhaps the best way to improve the quality of schools is to develop "from within" educational professionals the habits of cultivating our conceptual, reflective, virtuous repertoires together?

The question above highlights a third reflective inquiry topic, communicating the power of holistic journeys of understanding to colleagues and other stakeholders. Communication is a very challenging aspect of curriculum leadership. Trying to foster a generative, authentic culture among colleagues and stakeholders accustomed to standardization and management is a daunting task without easy answers. Such conversations are particularly challenging when concrete decisions of practice are at stake and there is an imbalance of positional authority, which is often the case in collegial conversations. Within the culture of management, which is the dominant culture, authority trumps understanding. Imagining Dorothy and Cindy in the role of administrative leaders or supervisors, we acknowledge that our efforts to embody respect for their interests and experiences may not be reciprocated. Under such circumstances, it is important to avoid becoming discouraged. But we can learn through experiences where relationships have blatant "power over" and authoritative dynamics or morph into them. In the realities of our dominant culture, sometimes all one can do is follow Voltaire's advice and tend our own garden.

The teaching, modeling, and communicating inquiries are informed by ongoing deliberative conversations. For example, the ongoing dialogue with our imaginary colleagues throughout the fourfolds provides an illustration of advancing holistic 3S pedagogy through reflective inquiry and deliberative conversation. Careful considerations of educational issues in which we examine, critique, and respond to our educational actions and interpretations are key characteristics of the deliberative spirit we have tried to portray. From the perspective of generative lead-learning, equalizing resources or positional authority are mere instrumental maneuvers of working toward equity. The more expansive aim of cultivating our capabilities is about providing meaningful opportunities to realize substantive freedoms (Sen, 2000). Toward this end, Nussbaum (2011) asks us two questions: "What are people actually able to do and to be? What real opportunities are available to them?" (p. x). Generative lead-learning provides individuals with opportunities to function in ways that they value and have reason to value. How might we reorganize our schools to be places of pluralistic humanism? How might we come together, young and old, to become more capable of living the lives we want?

The third repertoire is the *virtuous repertoire*. The virtuous repertoire is about refining one's capacity to make democratically wise practical decisions in educational contexts. Aristotle's golden mean reminds us to maintain a moderate and humble stance in the world. So too do other wisdom traditions that have been part of human history. Conceptually, this is demonstrated by the interpretation of critical pragmatism underpinning this book. Teachers must critically distance themselves from the unhelpful elements of dominant discourses and practices, while at the same time pragmatically move forward in an imperfect situation. We are continuously learning through experiences; and virtuous experiential learning embodies a love of knowledge, firmness, courage and caution, autonomy, generosity and culminates with a cultivation of practical wisdom. Regulations and structures can provide helpful guidelines; however, it is imperative for pedagogical artists to know when, why and how it is sometimes necessary to bend the rules (Schwartz & Sharpe, 2010).

PARTING THOUGHTS

How might we reorganize our schools in ways that temper the forces of authority, hierarchy, control, rules, and incentives? How might we make a democratic values and a love of wisdom a fundamental principles around which reorganize ourselves? Education is an endeavor that involves the complexities of being human. And generative lead-learning beckons us to use our imaginative, creatives powers and critical thinking to reorganizing ourselves in more humane, pluralistic ways. Ways that are not for the purpose of the production of uniformity but for authentic, inclusive communities that nurture our capacities for pedagogical artistry. All of our voices and contributions matter. Our choices, beliefs, and feelings matter. Our relationships, differences, and ethical commitments matter. Being lead-learner means that we strive together; no one should feel like they need to work alone in isolation.

Pause and Ponder

- How might I/we engage more fully with *lead-learning*?
- How might I/we *invite* other educational stakeholders to engage in deliberative conversations and reflective inquiry about holistic, democratic understanding and pedagogical artistry?
- How might I/we *create* and *sustain spaces* for *democratic* dialogue and *holistic understanding*?
- How am I/we doing with making sense of a *conceptual, reflective, and vitreous repertoires* that are paramount to holistic understanding and pedagogical artistry?

DELVING DEEPER: STUDY RESOURCES

Below we leave a set of offerings that have informed our thinking on the generative lead-learning fold. Again, these resources may not directly use the label of generative lead-learning, but we have found their contents thought-provoking in various ways. As you keep reading, we highly encourage you to find connects to resources you have encountered that you feel resonate with generative lead-learning and the other folds in this book.

Joseph, P. B. (Ed). (2000). *Cultures of curriculum* (2nd ed.). Mahwah, NJ: Lawrence Erlbaum Associates.

In this edited volume, the underlying belief systems and practices of a variety of curriculum orientations are thoroughly examined. This is a must read for understanding the dynamic relationship between curriculum and culture.

Nussbaum, M. C. (2011). *Creating capabilities: The human development approach.* Cambridge, MA: Belknap Press.
This is an accessible text that introduces an alternative theory of development. With numerous illustrative examples, Nussbaum explains a capabilities approach, as a more expansive lens through which we can apprehend development.

Noddings, N. (2013). *Education and democracy in the 21st century.* New York, NY: Teachers College Press.
In this book, one of the leading educational philosophers in the United States, Nel Noddings, explores various facets of democratic education. Written almost a century after Dewey's *Democracy and Education*, Noddings's analysis captures extraordinary historical detail, provides nuanced conceptual explanations, and offers her readers a vision for democratic education in the twenty-first century.

Schwartz, B., & Sharpe, K. (2010). *Practical wisdom: The right way to do the right thing.* New York, NY: Riverhead Books.
Schwartz and Sharpe are not speaking exclusively to teachers. However, they offer an incredibly insightful, yet accessible, book on practical wisdom from an Aristotelian perspective. This is an excellent book for readers who are frustrated with having important professional endeavors organized around rules and incentives.

REFERENCES

Henderson, J. G., et al. (2015). *Reconceptualizing curriculum development: Inspiring and informing action.* New York, NY: Routledge.

Joseph, P. B. (2000). Conceptualizing curriculum. In P. B. Joseph, S. L. Bravmann, M. A. Windschitl, E. A. Mikel, & N. S. Green, *Cultures of curriculum* (pp. 1–14). Mahwah, NJ: Lawrence Erlbaum Associates.

Nussbaum, M. C. (2011). *Creating capabilities: The human development approach.* Cambridge, MA: Belknap Press.

Noddings, N. (2013). *Education and democracy in the 21st century.* New York, NY: Teachers College Press.

Schulman, L. S. (1986). Those who understand: Knowledge growth in teaching. *Educational Researcher, 15*(2), 4–14.

Schwartz, B., & Sharpe, K. (2010). *Practical wisdom: The right way to do the right thing.* New York, NY: Riverhead Books.

Sen, A. (2000). *Development as freedom.* Oxford: Oxford University Press.

Chapter Five

Participatory Evaluating

*How are we democratically reviewing the diversified expressive outcomes
and impacts of this pedagogical artistry?*

Evaluation is quite often considered the bottom line of so much that happens
around education, and more often than not, evaluation is framed as a mecha-
nism of accountability. Teachers are held liable under the auspice of working
toward more equitable outcomes, mainly through two evaluative mechanisms: rubrics of teacher effectiveness and students' scores on standardized
tests. While No Child Left Behind (NCLB) mandated standardized achievement tests administered at the state-level, Race to the Top (RttT) incentivized
the implementation of state teacher evaluations systems. Moreover, accredita-
tion bodies have encouraged teacher educators to utilize standardized instruments in teacher preparation programs. A very current example of this can
be seen with the American Association of Colleges for Teacher Education's
(AACTE) Educational Teacher Performance Assessment (EdTPA), which is
becoming increasingly prevalent in schools of education, lauded as an impar-
tial evaluative tool. Thus, allegedly objective evaluative measures structure
teachers' preparation, daily practices as well as their pedagogical goals. Many
educators will likely have a frame of reference for how the dominate culture
illustrates results from standardized evaluation instruments. Bar graphs, line
graphs, pie charts, and other formats are staples for representing quantitative
data, and the image to come is a generic example of this.

Think back to the discussion in chapter 3 around the standardized-
management consciousness. The realm of evaluating with education seems to
be getting tethered evermore tightly to such consciousness. Standardized trajectories for evaluation play out in multifaceted ways. For example, student
readiness, professional competency, and processes of curriculum formation

ANNUAL PROFICIENT PERCENTAGE: 6TH GRADE

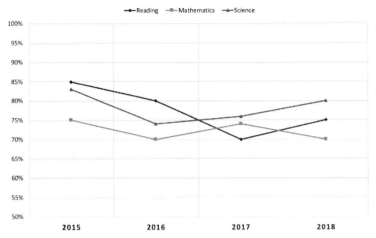

Figure 5.1.   Standardized Evaluation

are simplified via rubrics identifying clearly defined linear progress. As a powerful structure historically embedded in educational institutions, these are prefabricated paths toward "progress" but are more often than not taken for granted and not critically questioned. Inherent in standardized forms of evaluation also is the perpetuation of a semi-professional view of teachers. Take standardized testing as an example. This evaluation tool sends the message that teachers do not possess the ability to create assessments for students and assess learning. Instead testing companies become the ones given the authority to create the tests. And let us not overlook the profits they make from having schools use their evaluation tools. Thus, with metrics being devised through systems of bureaucratic control, teachers are predominantly encouraged to passively comply with regulations, instead of engage in their profession as the supreme art for advancing democratic ways of living.

Many scholars have provided a wide range of important critiques of standardized assessments and the consequences of the overuse of standardized achievement tests (Apple, 2011; Au, 2011; Pinar, 2013; Tienken, 2017). Here, our concerns focus on three trends in educational evaluation that are particularly undemocratic. The first issue is one of logical reductionism. Students' achievement are reduced to their performances on standardized tests. The complexities of teaching are concurrently reduced to the outcomes of such tests and a set of observable behaviors. Moreover, curriculum, teaching, and leadership studies are reduced to overly simplistic and prefabricated formulations of what constitutes effective educational practice. Curriculum is diminished from a complicated conversation to prescribed lists of behavioral objectives, materials, and scope and sequence charts. The inherently moral and political aspects of teaching are overlooked when definitions of success are restricted to measureable transference of knowledge. Rooted in its scientific management heritage, leadership loses its democratic sensibility when pigeonholed by a management mindset.

Our second, albeit closely related, set of concerns involves the cold aesthetic that permeates the dominant discourse of educational evaluation. Yearning to claim objectivity, proponents of standardization advance a discourse that separates value judgments and technical decisions. As such, allegedly objective systems of evaluation are ironically discussed as a value neutral enterprise. However, the etymology of the word "objective" is telling. Parker Palmer (1993) explains, "the Latin root of objective means to put against, to oppose" and continues that, "in German its literal translation is standing-over-againstness" (p. 87). Beyond reducing journeys of understanding to accounting for measurable learning outcomes and behavioral objectives, a violent ethos is imposed through the dominant evaluative discourse. Individualism is put against ecological or communitarian perspectives. Instead of fostering cooperative relationships, embracing dissensus, complexity and uncertainty, so-called objective evaluation encourages competition, uniformity, and control. According to Palmer, "it has made us adversaries of ourselves" (p. 88).

Third, we are troubled by the imposition of centralized and distant sources of authority circulated by the dominant discourse of educational evaluation. Educational practitioners, including those who work at universities, find themselves caught up in and encouraged to reproduce what Michel Foucault (1980) called a power situation. Put straightforwardly, educational imaginations are discouraged by mechanisms of evaluation and quality improvement. As examples, EdTPA, numerous variations of Danielson's (2007) framework for effective teaching, and politicians' general obsession with raising students standardized test scores simplify and disembody expressions of pedagogical artistry in profoundly undemocratic ways. Teachers and students alike, including teacher educators, are objectified by evaluative systems where the value of every course of action is only validated by its measured consequence.

Participatory evaluating stands as a vivid contrast through its embrace of the complexities and ambiguities of human experience. Education as experience is a deeply personal and contextual phenomena. If teachers are on journeys of understanding marked by continuous growth and broadening of intellectual horizons, a more expansive form of evaluation is required. Put differently, participatory evaluating is a multi-vocal effort to appraise the qualitative dimensions of our growth from within. Such evaluating is also connected with the other three folds.

How are thing going in relation to purposeful awakening? How are teachers becoming attuned to their vocational calling in meaningful ways and leading students to explore their own vocational callings as well? In what ways are transactional relationships between teachers and students taking place through creative teaching practices that embody holistic 3S pedagogy? Moreover, in what sense are efforts to enhance educational experiences buoyed by generative lead-learning? How are curriculum leaders inviting diversified perspectives and disciplined study?

A DELIBERATIVE CONVERSATION

In light of the disparate points of view we have been illustrating, there is also a strong, unifying point of agreement. We share with Dorothy and Cindy a dedication to educational excellence and commitments to disciplined problem solving. Put differently, we all want *good* schools and strongly believe that our professional responsibilities call upon us to *improve* the current conditions of schools and classrooms. However, these evaluative dimensions are complicated. Efforts to improve educational practice, rest on how one frames what constitutes a *good* education. This becomes our point of departure, as our dialogue with Dorothy and Cindy continues.

Dorothy: *All this democracy talk is all fine and good in theory, but we all know that at the end of the day educators are expected to show evidence of results. In the real world, all of this talk doesn't matter. It's just not practical because the kids are going to take their tests, and we have face the facts. Either we have been successful as educators or we have not. The truth is in the data.*

Cindy: *Of course we should be held accountable, Dorothy, but I have to say that I know how my students will do before I see their test score data. Assessment should be happening every day!*

Dorothy: *Well sure, that is a good point. I think our schools have done a really nice job of recognizing that. As you know, we don't just do assessment on test days. The academic coaches and specialists have done a really good job of developing common unit assessments and choosing value-added measures. All these are helpful for tracking learning and progress.*

Cindy: *And, building off of that, some of the PLCs have done really amazing work using backward design. The whole process begins with designing assessments. What are the deeper, higher-order understandings we want our students to master? If we are designing good assessments in PLCs, we will have a pretty good idea about how the tests will turn out.*

Dorothy: *That's good, but we all know that PLCs are a whole lot of extra stuff, Cindy. And time presents such limitations on what we all can do. I am mostly concerned with the hard data. It gives us objective truth about what is happen-*

ing. Numbers don't lie. I wouldn't want to discourage what teachers are doing in PLCs, but I would insist on them showing me that it is working. The only way to know whether it is working is by looking at the data.

Cindy: *I know that it is important to look at objective data. It can be very helpful in terms of assessment, but you can know a lot about students' progress by looking at teacher-generated assessments too. Especially, if the assessments are done well and authentically, you will get a lot of information about students' thought processes and level of thinking on Bloom's taxonomy.*

Dorothy: *I'm just saying that when the state rates my school and all of my teachers, they aren't going to be talking about Bloom's taxonomy. And they surely aren't going to be interested in looking through piles and piles of teacher-generated assessments from my school nor all the schools in the state. It's just not practical. They are going to look at our hard data, and then, they will compare us to all of the schools around us. I just want our schools to do well that's what it comes down to.*

Cindy: *But, as educators, isn't deep understanding of content our ultimate purpose? Content knowledge is absolutely fundamental. The states are tuned into this too, I think. They spend a lot of time, energy, and funding articulating content knowledge standards, and our educators spend a lot too studying and thinking about teaching content.*

Dorothy: *I know . . . I know . . . It's just important to remember that we are not self-employed. You might think something is important, I might think something else is important. A group of teachers might sit down in a PLC and say something completely different should be the enduring understanding for a set of content standards. What really matters is what the state says we need to be teaching our students. After all, they are the one's who are assessing us!*

Dan: *What about other stakeholders though? I appreciate that there is a need to attend to the state accountability system. It's highly likely that it's not going away anytime soon. Also, Cindy, I hear an emphasis on teachers' points of view in what you are saying, which is a really important point on evaluation. Shouldn't children, families, and community perspectives be considered in the process of evaluation?*

Cindy: *That is what I think I am trying to encourage with UbD and authentic assessments. I want teachers to be child-centered and culturally responsive. That is our job as educators.*

Jen: *Dan, please correct me if I am wrong here, but Cindy . . . I think he is speaking on something a little different than just teachers knowing about students and families and letting that inform assessment. While educators do need to do assessments, how might we more actively involve students, families, and community members with evaluating? Why should only teachers and the state have the final say in the progress of learning? What about the students' points* *of view on their own learning; why do we don't weigh their opinions as equals? What about families and community members getting involved in assessing us?*

Dorothy: *The state will report to all of us and let us know how we are doing. If our scores are low, families know. I think that accountability to the state department is accountability to families. They can access the data reports and see for themselves how things are going in the school, with the teachers, and with their kids. It has to be this way. Most parents don't know how to evaluate their schools on their own.*

UNPACKING THE COLLEGIAL EXCHANGE

Who ought to evaluate the quality of educational courses of action, and on what grounds and for what purposes should such evaluative processes take place? Illustrated above, we see any answer to these questions is multifaceted and contentious. To be sure, the current and well-established method of evaluating the effectiveness of a teacher, course, program, or school is standardized assessments. Educators in K-12 public schools have grown accustomed to state-mandated achievement tests. A uniform and quantified representation of "achievement" provides an unambiguous value to the given educational course of action. Recall Dorothy's comment that numbers do not lie. In a university setting, students provide a monolithic appraisal of curriculum and teaching through course evaluations.

While the source and quantified outcomes of such reports is straightforward, the purpose is vague. Standardized tests in K-12 schools are mandated by states in accordance with federal policy guidelines; and often, the quantified outcomes of course evaluations at the universities are derived solely from students' responses. Are the K-12 tests quality assurance measures or governmental control mechanisms? Are undergraduate or graduate students' feedback evaluations of the quality and rigor of the content and procedures of a given course, or is it simply a customer service survey? Ideally, one would like to assume that evaluative tools can inform the improvement of curriculum and instruction. However, it is naive to presume the dominant methods of evaluation do not also carry out other functions.

For a number of reasons, the awakening, teaching, and lead-learning advanced in the previous three folds call for a more expansive, inclusive, and flexible method of evaluation. First, we are not merely interested in specific and predictable outcomes of educational experiences, such as the acquisition of particular sets of knowledge and skills. Though, of course, such outcomes are often worthwhile. We are also deeply invested in and interested in long-term *personal, interpersonal, institutional, community,* and *societal impacts.*

Put differently, we encourage stakeholders to evaluate educational endeavors with reference to not only what can be immediately measured, but also the enduring value of the experience. Indeed, often times the enduring value of an educational endeavor is ineffable, realized well after the experience and difficult to account for beforehand.

Notice how Dorothy and Cindy are locked into the dominant interpretation of accountability. As such they are following a logical pattern that began in chapter 3 with their exclusive focus on the technical qualities of educational purposes. Moving forward to chapter 4, they value efficient and effective methods for transmitting prescribed content standards to students who do learning. Dorothy and Cindy seem to think questioning the democratic value of those content standards to be outside of the scope of their professional role and responsibility. However, there is a subtle difference between our two colleagues' perspectives regarding matters of methods.

Dorothy consistently looks upward in her bureaucratic chain of command for authoritative answers of how to teach as well as what to teach. It is noteworthy that she identifies the state content standards, the rubric for the state teacher evaluation system, and now in this fold the state-mandated achievement tests as her basis for knowing what to do and how well it is being done. Although she does not disagree with Dorothy, Cindy upholds a less rigid viewpoint. Cindy uncritically accepts the state standards as the fundamental authority of what should be taught. Nonetheless, she looks to a wider range of authoritative voices to inform how education ought to be carried out—embodying and reinforcing Tienken's point about an autocratic meritocracy. Sharing Dorothy's persistent valuing of efficiency and effectiveness, leads Cindy to particular forms of educational research. Looking to researchers who construct strategies or programs that "work," Cindy attempts to broaden the craft reflection exuded by Dorothy. Drawing on their shared habituated values—that is, technical effectiveness and efficiency—Cindy tries to persuade her colleague to consider how implementing various "best practice" arguments might be the most successful strategy for improving measureable goals.

Unfortunately, the values of technical efficiency and effectiveness fall flat in considerations of democratic virtue. In other words, both Dorothy and Cindy have not been engaged in reflecting on the value-laden aspects of their practice. For example, when she was an elementary school principal, Dorothy might begin with a common learning objective such as, "Students will be able to identify the initial sound, medial and final sound of one-syllable words." She might insist that all kindergarten and first grade teachers include this skill in their lesson plans and utilize PLCs, and she, or another designated administrative figure, would use evaluative walkthroughs to ensure that this skill is being taught in classrooms. Dorothy's efforts would be rounded out with an examination of standardized test data with particular focus on items that assess this particular skill. Nowhere in this process did Dorothy pause to question *why* identifying phonemes in this manner is an essential skill for children in these grade levels; if we were to ask her why not, she would likely say it is not within her role and responsibility to know this. Her role is to make sure it is being done in the classroom and students are learning it.

Meanwhile, Cindy might begin by incorporating this same learning objective into a consideration of broader educational goals. She, for example, might emphasize the importance of identifying phonemes as part of developing young readers' phonemic awareness. Then, working as an instructional coach, she might also remind her colleagues phonemic awareness is one key component of comprehensive reading instruction. Suggesting that becoming competent readers influences learning in other content areas, Cindy might further suggest interdisciplinary instruction be planned in PLCs. However, within neither of these explanations would Dorothy nor Cindy be engaging in aims talking.

As we saw, aims talking is a central feature of the professional awakening fold with salience to the participatory evaluating fold. Nel Noddings (2013) explains, "We point to aims when we are asked, or ask ourselves, why we are engaged in certain activities and why we are committed to certain beliefs and practices" (p. 40). This is crucial for generating democratic virtues. How do the activities we are carrying out in classrooms as well as the beliefs that underlie those practices tie into freedom and flourishing, the central aims of life? We (Jim, Jen, and Dan) are asking a markedly different evaluative question than Dorothy and Cindy. Whereas Dorothy wants to see evidence of measurable skill attainment and Cindy wants to see demonstrations of deeper subject matter understanding, we are concerned with how this subject matter understanding is embedded in holistic 3S understanding, virtues conducive to democracy as a moral way of living. To be clear, we are not criticizing our colleagues efforts to teach this particular literacy skill. Rather, we are inviting reflective inquiry and deliberative conversation into the matter of how we might endeavor to teach important skills with an enduring sense of practical wisdom. How might a skill in content knowledge be taught and evaluated with attention given to both democratic self and social understandings?

What would participatory evaluating look like? We envision a diverse range of stakeholders reviewing teachers' and students' journeys of understanding expressed through multiple forms of representation. Participatory evaluating contrasts Dorothy's focus on state-mandated standardized testing and Cindy's commitment to predetermined performances of subject matter understanding constructed by local teams of educators. First, instead of a customary form of evaluation being conducted exclusively by positional authorities, we are advancing an inclusive participatory process. Consistent with the open-minded and open-hearted approaches to aims talking, holistic pedagogical enactments, and generative lead-learning deliberative conversation is the heart of participatory evaluating. The insights of bureaucratic or expert authority figures are honored and put into dialogue with students, families, community members, scholars-researchers, disciplinary specialists, and other stakeholders. Moreover, facilitating an authentic dialogue inclusive to the various qualities of educational experience observed and valued by these diverse stakeholders requires freedom of expression. Rather than the uniformity of standardized or common forms of evaluation, participatory evaluating embraces the creativity of distinct and novel responses of disparate values coming together for the emergence of democratic virtues.

PAUSE, REFLECT, AND IMAGINE POSSIBILITIES

Reflect on an educational experience with a special teacher who impacted your life in a substantial and lasting way. Do you think you could fully articulate the significance of that teacher's impact on your life in the moment of the experience? Are there aspects that you can better explain with the benefit of hindsight and continued reflection? Now, imagine yourself actualizing your vocational calling with your future students. Is it reasonable to ask you to predict, with exacting detail, how your and your students' behaviors will unfold? Would you be able to make such precise and meaningful predictions that someone in positional authority could or should hold you accountable for ensuring the behaviors you forecasted occur as anticipated?

Many dedicated teachers we know express educational aims that are not so easily calculated and quantified. For example, it is not uncommon for teachers at elementary schools to want their students to "fall in love with reading or math"; or for a high school teachers to want their students to "gain a deep appreciation" for their disciplinary content. These deeper aims transpire in countless ways and are often deeply personal. For some students through that love of reading may never happen, they may learn to do it but never read novels or poetry on their own time. Suggesting uniformity among students' responses would be facile. Moreover, imposing one's predilections on other's experiences, not to mention the meaning and methods by which they choose to express the meaning they ascribe to those experiences, would be domineering.

For example, as co-authors of this book, we share a commitment to realizing the practical utility of educational theory. Additionally, we hope to provoke such an interest among our readers. However, our journeys of understanding are as variable as our personal and professional experiences. Is this not also the case among our readerships? We readily acknowledge that outcomes of reading this book here and now are unique and foreseeable.

We advanced fourfolds. Likely, you can name them. The meaning, value, and utility of the four folds in your daily teaching, curriculum, and leadership activities is more appropriately addressed as an open-ended set of questions: What does the content of this book mean to you as a practicing educator? Will it broaden or deepen your study and practice into your professionals artistry? How so? Why? And when? What might you not be able to resonate with now but revisit certain ideas in a year, five, maybe even ten, and how might your takeaways vary?

The distinctions between participatory evaluating and the more prevalent modes of evaluation, illustrated by Dorothy and Cindy, are three-pronged. Dorothy and Cindy envisage immediate of outcomes that are expressed consistently among all participants. Hence, their evaluative process begins first with predetermined expectations held with certainty. Before the journey begins, they have a set answer about what they hope to successfully accomplish. Second, their journey ensues with the transmission of presumably essential knowledge, skills and dispositions. Along the way, their assessments might indicate that students and/or colleagues are not meeting expectations, to which they will follow up with remediation. Third, the evaluative process is organized around matters of positional authority. Being in charge is equated to understanding. Consequently, teachers and other stakeholders are marginalized, as authority figures are elevated as more informed or powerful cultural gates keepers. These bureaucratic proclivities are exactly what we hope to disrupt and reimagine in this book.

As we envision it, participatory evaluating differs from traditional educational evaluation in each of these three ways. Evaluation is seen as having a more expansive purpose, including immediate outcomes but also long-term impacts of educational enterprises. As such, only certain achievements can be anticipated. An "all things considered" approach to evaluating also sets out to recognize and appreciate the idiosyncratic, unanticipated achievements of a course of study. Understanding education as a transactional experience, instead of the transferring of knowledge, signifies that the complexities and unpredictability of human affairs are embraced, rather than simplified. What is more, it is important to note that most educational evaluation is not participatory in nature. Thus, participatory evaluating is a departure from traditional authority-based evaluative processes, like the suggestions articulated by Dorothy and Cindy. Evaluation, from our point of view, is about more than imposing authoritative guidelines. It is, following Eisner, a means through which we can educate the public.

We envision evaluation taking on a pedagogical function rather than a solely bureaucratic one. Educational outcomes and impacts are pluralistic and can only be meaningfully captured through multiple forms of representation. Accordingly, evaluation (if it is participatory) is not a solitary activity. Can we imagine the expectations Dorothy finds within her institutional hierarchy and the standards Cindy knows through her professional organizations were enhanced by the discussion and debate of various stakeholders? What if evaluation were approached democratically, where children's points of view are taken as seriously as central office administrators? Of course, this is not to say that stakeholders hold the same knowledge. The disparate experiences of various stakeholders—students, families, community members, teachers, support staff and administrators—offer different knowledge and ways of perceiving the qualities of teaching and learning. Participatory evaluating calls for a democratically inclusive dialogue; because each stakeholder's knowledge is not merely unique, but irreplaceable.

What makes the participatory evaluating incredibly intriguing and potentially very powerful is that it goes against the grain of so many of the trends and entrenched habits around evaluation in education. Educational evaluation is heavily informed by an abundance of quantitative data. But what about honoring the qualitative dimensions and qualitative data of education as well? When trying to find ways to express concrete illustrations of what participatory evaluation might look and feel like in real life, we admit that it has not been a simple exercise for us. In lieu of generate an imagine for participatory evaluation, we instead want point share two examples, which draw on Jen's experiences in the arts. Participatory evaluation is a natural fit with portfolios and galleries.

Portfolios are by no means a new form of evaluation. They commonly get a nod in pedagogical literature as tools to use as a form of summative assessment. When was the last time you used portfolios in your classroom? Or when was the last time you created a portfolio of your own learning? Generally speaking, a portfolio is a collection of evidence on an individual's experience, efforts, and progress of learning over time. Portfolios can be done on a large scale (e.g., over a semester or year) or a small scale (e.g., a mini-portfolio). The collection of artifacts for a portfolio is always purposefully done and a key characteristic is depth, that is, to provide a comprehensive illustration of learning.

Artifacts, records, or recordings of students' performances of understandings and students' work samples might be included to illustrate journeys of growth and understanding. Portfolios can be full of hard copies of documents, or perhaps even electronic. Some items in the portfolio might be selected by the teacher, while others are chosen by the student. Standardized test scores might be included as one representation of student understanding but do not stand alone as more important than other classroom artifacts. Additionally, there might be letters or statements by the students about their work and learning. Other possibilities might be self-reflective and -evaluative statements, peer reflections and evaluations, logs, journals, and diaries, electronic audio and visual recordings, and photographs. Portfolios might even contain teachers' reflective and evaluative statements.

But let us not think portfolios are not limited to the classroom and students' learning. Portfolios can show us needs that emerge and can help us think of future steps in our learning. What might it look like if teachers were encouraged to create professional portfolios that were taken seriously and used in the evaluation of their practice? What if teachers and students created portfolios about the learning in their class and then sought ways to share it with other educational stakeholders? The idea of sharing with others brings us to the second concrete possibility for thinking about participatory evaluating: galleries or exhibits.

Galleries, or exhibits, are another sort collection of artifacts and also places those forms of expression on display for others to have experiences with. An exhibit can have a theme or at other times be dedicated to showing an individual or group of individuals' artifacts. Let us pretend for a moment that you come with us to an art exhibit. What might the experience be like for us? How might our learning unfold? Galleries are spaces that invite dialogue and can be experienced both independently and communally. Not only will each of us have our own experience in the gallery with the artworks, but we will also have the opportunity for a shared experience with each other in the space. Our conversations about our various interpretations and appraisals of the displays can become part of the experience. What if our schools and departments of education became sites where we celebrate and exhibit holistic understanding? What if schools were places where we invite a variety of educational stakeholders to engage with, respond to, and evaluate how we are doing with cultivating holistic understandings?

We can hear the statements starting to play in the minds of some educators like "All of that sounds great, but who has the time and resources to do such things?" "If the test is what ends up mattering the most, why bother with alternatives?" "Having so many type of artifacts seems okay, but how are we going to do an objective evaluation of learning?" While such sentiments express valid concerns, we also need to realize that we are continuing to perpetuate the dominant paradigm when we use such responses. Participatory evaluating is about working together and finding ways of reimagining, rethinking, and recreating what we think about evaluation, how it is done, and whose voices are part of the process of making judgments about learning. Portfolio and galleries are just two possibilities; what others are there that might yet be created or explored?

PARTING THOUGHTS

Participatory evaluating is an inclusive process of noticing, acknowledging, and representing stakeholders' diverse insights. At the heart of participatory evaluating is pausing to appraise on how things are going. We can take stock from our own viewpoint, but we also cannot forget the participatory dimension. Many voices are welcome at the table and are listened to and respected. Diverse points of view are acknowledged and deliberated upon. Are we broadening our interpretations of *what* education is all about? How are we doing with critically distancing and disrupting oppressive structures in education? As we broaden our horizons through diversified inquiries and deliberative conversations, are we unlearning problematic habits and re-educating each other's perceptions of holistic, democratic understanding? How might each of these three facets of evaluating—that is noticing, acknowledging, and representing—be a democratically inclusive process? We encourage you imagine this fashion of evaluating.

Pause and Ponder

As we come to a close here with the fourth fold in the fourfold process, here is our open set of questions for contemplation. May these questions be points of departure of thinking by yourself and hopefully with other educational stakeholders.

- How are we doing with reviewing and critiquing our work as pedagogical artists?
- How are we doing with *educating the public* to the power of 3S pedagogical artistry?
- How are we doing with inviting *broader community/public* to encounter and engage with expressions of 3S pedagogical artistry from our schools and classrooms?
- How are we doing with *peer-reviewing activities* through diverse forms of representation?
- How am I/are we doing with the professional awakening, holistic teaching, and generative lead-learning?

DELVING DEEPER: STUDY RESOURCES

Below we leave a set of offerings that have informed our thinking on the participatory evaluating fold. Again, these resources may not directly use the label of participatory evaluating, but we have found their contents thought-provoking in various ways. As you keep reading, we highly encourage you to find connects to resources you have encountered that you feel resonate with the features of participatory evaluating and the other folds in this book.

Eisner, E. W. (1994). *The educational imagination: On the design and evaluation of school programs* (3rd ed.). New York, NY: Macmillan.
Eisner, E. W. (2004). *The arts and the creation of mind.* New Haven, CT: Yale University Press.
Eisner, E. W. (2017). *The enlightened eye: Qualitative inquiry and the enhancement of educational practice* (2nd ed.). New York, NY: Teachers College Press.

As has been made evident throughout several chapters of this text, it is difficult to exaggerate the Elliot Eisner's influence on this book. Eisner's work helps to transform the ways educators think about research, evaluation, and curriculum. He wrote prolifically and with great profundity offering, among other contributions, an advancement of the arts as a rigorous way of knowing about educational endeavors. He also encourages us to examine the ideologies underpinning what we do in school and why. The three books mentioned above, *The Educational Imagination*, *The Arts and the Creation of Mind*, and *The Enlightened Eye,* are great places to begin delving deeper into participatory evaluating and beyond.

Schwandt, T. A. (2015). *Evaluation foundations revisited: Cultivating a life of the mind for practice.* Stanford, CA: Stanford University Press.

Thomas Schwandt is a leading scholar in the field of educational evaluation. Operating out of a hermeneutic perspective, Schwandt's views on evaluation were particularly helpful for conceptualizing the participatory evaluating fold. For a nuanced and "all things considered" approach to evaluation, this book is an excellent resource.

REFERENCES

Apple, M. (2011). *Education and power.* New York, NY: Routledge.
Au, W. (2011). Teaching under the new Taylorism: high-stakes testing and the standardization of the 21st century curriculum. *Journal of Curriculum Studies, 43*(1), 25–45.

Foucault, M. (1980). *Power/knowledge: Selected interviews and other writings, 1972–1977.* C. Gordon (Ed.). New York, NY: Random House.

Noddings, N. (2013). *Education and democracy in the 21st century.* New York, NY: Teachers College Press.

Palmer, P. J. (1993). *To know as we are known: Education as a spiritual journey.* San Francisco, CA: HarperCollins.

Pinar, W. F. (2013). *Curriculum studies in the United States: Present circumstances, intellectual histories.* New York, NY: Palgrave Macmillan.

Tienken, C. H. (2017). *Defying Standardization: Creating curriculum for an uncertain future.* Lanham, MD: Rowman & Littlefield.

Epilogue

We begin our epilogue with a quote taken from Maxine Greene's response to an edited collection of essays celebrating her productive career as an educational philosopher and art education activist. This quote, which captures the essence of Greene's "love of wisdom," touches on the heart and soul of the problem solving we are advancing. Our fourfold process is deeply grounded in the existential artistry that she celebrates; Greene is an inspirational model for the journey of understanding embedded in the fourfold process.

Because Greene's philosophical aesthetics—her feel for authentic democratic living—so exemplifies and personifies the aesthetic dimensions of this text, we quote her at some length. Greene (1998) writes:

> I ponder my own memories as I think about the past and present—and (even now) [wonder] what I am not yet. Have I simply been a good student? Have I been lucky enough to be visited by inspiration—at least now and then? Saying this, I am reminded of the Nobel Lecture written by the Polish poet, Wistawa Szymborska. Exploring the meanings of inspiration, [Szymborska] reminded us that it is not the exclusive privilege of poets or artists:
>
>> There is, there has been, there will always be a certain group of people whom inspiration visits. It's made up of all those who've consciously chosen their calling and do their job with love and imagination. It may include doctors, teachers, gardeners—I could list a hundred more professions. Their work becomes one continuous adventure so long as they manage to keep discovering new challenges in it. Difficulties and setbacks never quell their curiosity. A swarm of new questions emerges from every problem they solve. Whatever inspiration is, it's born from a continuous "I don't know." [Szymborska (1996)]. (p. 256)

Greene (1998) then goes on to explain why she selected Szymborska's "I don't know" phrase as a fitting metaphor for her philosophical vocation:

> Teaching, writing, speaking, looking at paintings, watching plays and dance performances, listening to music, reading (always reading), I know the challenges are always new. The questions still gather, and I relish my sense of incompleteness. I can only live, it seems to me, with a consciousness of possibility, of what might be, of what *ought* to be. Looking back, I attribute my choosing of questions to my being a woman (and a wife and mother), to my involvement with literature and the other arts, to the persisting conversations with students, to my friendships, and to my awareness of the darkness, of the silence that greets, or longing for some cosmic meaning, for a "truth." (p. 256)

Greene's sense of adventuress not-knowing touches on the *hermeneutic humility* that we introduced in our theoretical platform chapter. It is a humility that is integrally linked to a faith in the power of democratic, holistic understanding.

This faith invites a number of deep professional questions for educators and for the societies in which they work. Greene's celebration of her holistic pursuit of understanding brings to mind Eisner's (2015) critical question concerning educational equity: "Can a more informed conception of what constitutes quality in education lead to greater equity for students and ultimately for the culture?" (p. 28). The context for Eisner's question is his call for inclusive educational evaluations that are respectful of diverse "forms of representation," and this interpretation of human diversity is a key normative referent in the participatory evaluating we are advancing. While practicing holistic teaching, can educators embrace the pluralistic literacy that Greene and Eisner champion? Through the practice of 3S pedagogical artistry, can educators open avenues for the emergence of their students' diverse vocational artistries? Can educators recognize that such educational diversity goes to the heart of democratic ethics and productivity? Can educators speak such pluralistic truth to management power?

The practice of the fourfold process foregrounds such tough critical questions, and we feel hopeful that there are many educators who are willing to thoughtfully undertake such challenges. Our hopefulness—our upbeat prognosis for the fourfold process—is heartened by our positive working relationships with a host of good-hearted, open-minded, and responsible educators who have contributed over many years to the creation of this book. These collegial engagements have occurred in both university-based graduate courses and school-based grant projects. In addition, we have been collaborating with a growing community of international educators who share our interest in integrating curriculum, teaching, and leadership studies (Castner, Schneider, & Henderson, 2017; Ulgins & Ylimaki, 2017).

In the theoretical platform chapter, we note the twenty-seven years of action research that inform this text's development, most recently the 2015–2018 teacher leadership grant funded by the Ohio Department of Education (ODE). This ODE grant work has been quite helpful in conceptualizing the fourfold process. We refined the fourfold process while working with thirty-nine teacher leaders in two public school districts in the Cleveland, Ohio metropolitan area. One of the school districts is located in a high socioeconomic status (SES) community, while the other district is located in a much lower SES community. Amid the challenges associated with the pervasive and dominating trends toward management standardization, we have documented and analyzed the many positive ways that motivated administrative and teacher leaders have demonstrated their desire and ability to work together to practice the fourfold process.

Our ODE grant work has generated a number of exciting products. One artifact coming out of the grant is a book—*Creating a Culture of Support for Teacher Leaders: A Vision for Change and Hope* (Gornik & Samford, in press)—in which administrative leaders in the two Ohio school districts present narratives on how they supported teachers' 3S pedagogical artistry.

We conclude our book by highlighting an ethical artifact from our grant work. Following an introductory study of the fourfold process, the thirty-nine teacher leaders in the two school districts were asked to reflect on their professional leadership ethics using the medical profession's Hippocratic oath as a normative referent. One of the teacher leaders composed the following statement of her ethical commitment to the study and practice of the fourfold process:

> I swear to fulfill to the best of my ability and judgment this covenant. Working as a lead learner, I will respect the artistry of democratic, holistic pedagogy as I respectively follow in the footsteps of committed past educators and as I advocate for equally committed current and future educators. I will fully respect our young learners, fellow teachers, families, and community stakeholders. I will remember that we are members of an aspiring democratic society with special obligations and responsibilities.
>
> Like John Dewey, I believe that our democratic, holistic pedagogy constitutes society's supreme professional artistry because our virtuous practices set the ethical, developmental, and lifelong learning stages for all other vocations and professions. I will continue my disciplined study towards a deeper understanding of democratic, holistic pedagogy; knowing that there is always more to learn. I recognize that my society, and particularly my students, deserve the best of my abilities to engage in—and to model—democratic practical wisdom. I believe in the enduring importance of democratic general education, and I aim to promote the skills and virtues that are needed in all of our society's vocations

and professions: self-sufficiency, creative problem solving, responsible inde-
pendence, respectful empathy, civil relations, and informed judgments.

I will remember that I do not teach a lesson plan, nor a reading deficiency,
but a human being whose skills may affect that student's future family and economic stability. My efforts will aim to teach the whole child and help that child
develop in mind and spirit. I believe that this is a basic democratic right for all
children in our society, rich or poor.

If I do not violate this oath, may I enjoy my life and my professional artistry—
respected while I live and remembered with affection thereafter. May I always
act so as to preserve the finest traditions of my supreme calling, and may I long
experience the joys of teaching those who seek my educational guidance and help.

This book is written for all of the good-hearted, open-minded, responsible
educators in the United States and around the world who might be inspired to
practice the fourfold process after an appropriate introduction. These educators, and their supportive curriculum stakeholders, are the future hope for the
problem-solving artistry advanced in this text.

The fourfold process is positioned at the intersection of critical theorizing
and practical artistry, and this is why critical pragmatism is one of the key
guiding principles of this curriculum leadership book. Enacting this critical
pragmatism through a humble pursuit of wise judgments is easier said than
done. It requires a courageous ethical perseverance in standardized management contexts. We recognize that teaching-to-the-test may be an appropriate
deliberative judgment in some pedagogical contexts. The problem we are
addressing in this book is not such informed decision-making. It is the doctrinaire enforcement of prescribed learning objectives, imposed curriculum
maps, and standardized tests. The focus of this book is on the enactment
of thoughtful pedagogical judgments that have enduring democratic value.
We want teachers to be able to "walk the talk" of their organization's mission statement. How many educational institutions proudly claim that their
workers teach to the test? As you ponder this question, consider Kent State
University's mission statement:

> The mission of Kent State University is to discover, create, apply, and share
> knowledge, as well as foster ethical and humanitarian values in the service of
> Ohio and the global community. As an eight-campus educational system, Kent
> State offers a broad array of academic programs to engage students in diverse
> learning environments that educate them to think critically and to expand their
> intellectual horizons while attaining the knowledge and skills necessary for
> responsible citizenship and productive careers.

Enacting such a mission statement requires an ethical fidelity that is actualized through a disciplined pursuit of professional excellence. This book advances one particular way to pursue this educational artistry.

We bring our book to a close by recognizing and encouraging our dedicated colleagues to remain vigilant to three potential pitfalls that can impede the pursuit of this text's professional excellence:

- **Pitfall 1:** Be aware of and resist the temptation to adopt a pre-given answer as a replacement for engaging in your own disciplined study and practice. Such answers are incredibly prevalent these days. In one's eagerness to "do well," readily available answers within dominant policy rhetoric and management discourses can provide an illusion of a "path of less resistance" and "the perfect pill to fix the ill." Remember democracy interpreted as a moral standard of living is inherently complex, and there is no substitute for critical thinking that is informed by a love of wisdom.
- **Pitfall 2:** Be aware of the possibility of wanting to give up and toss in the towel. When things do not work out smoothly, we sometimes simply say it is just too hard and cannot be done. This forfeits our sense of agency and sets up absolutes in our minds about our contexts, the educational stakeholders around us, and our futures. We also turn off our problem-solving capacities and generative instincts. We must not strive forward with blind optimism but with faith in the power of democratic, holistic human understanding. Persevere! Do not settle for undemocratic habits, traditions, and customs. Treat your classroom and life as an experiment by lighting an inspirational candle, not cursing the bureaucratic darkness.
- **Pitfall 3:** Be aware of dogmatism in any overt or covert form. A cautionary red flag should raise in your mind when ideas are expressed as undeniable and undisputable by people. The process of attending to diverse and, at times, competing viewpoints in generative and generous ways is greatly hindered by doctrinaire dispositions and structures. Democratic ways of living cannot be coerced and require a non-doctrinaire stance in the world. Remember that this book's interpretation of professional leadership is invitational in nature and that hermeneutic humility lies at the heart of democratic virtues. It is always okay to pose questions, to not be certain, to disagree, and to change our minds. Faithfully carrying out democratic virtues is always a "power-within" and "power-with" endeavor.

This book points to the possibility of a paradigmatic shift in education from practicing standardized judgments to pursuing democratic practical wisdom. Such a fundamental change in orientation begins with the kind of motivated educational leaders that we have experienced in our ODE grant work. Based on our extensive collaborative work with a wide range of teachers and educational administrators, we—the three co-authors of this text—think that such educational leadership has substantial growth potential. In fact, we think this leadership already exists, albeit in intuitive, small-scale, and informal ways.

We believe that there are many educators who are ready to embrace the study and practice of the fourfold process. We celebrate their sense of professionalism; and given the numerous threats to our planet's democratic future, the time is urgent to identify and nurture this educational artistry.

We are asking educators, together with their engaged educational stakeholders, to imagine with us the future practice of an enlightened educational problem solving for societies with democratic aspirations. We invite educators to join us in practicing this text's "educational imagination" (Eisner, 1994). Citing Benjamin Franklin, Luce (2017) notes that, "the price of liberty is eternal vigilance"; and he warns that, "when a culture stops looking to the future, it loses a vital force" (pp. 203–4). We strongly feel that the practice of the fourfold process is a key way to the bright future of global democratic vitality.

REFERENCES

Castner, D., Schneider, J., & Henderson, J. (2017). Advancing an ethic of curriculum-based teacher leadership. *Leadership and Policy in Schools, 16*(2), 328–56.

Eisner, E. W. (1994). *The educational imagination: On the design and evaluation of school programs* (3rd ed.). New York, NY: Macmillan.

———. (2015). What does it mean to say a school is doing well? In A. C. Ornstein, E. F. Pajak, & S. B. Ornstein (Eds.), *Contemporary issues in curriculum* (6th ed., pp. 21–29). Boston, MA: Pearson.

Gornik, R., & Samford, W. L. (In press). *Creating a culture of support for teacher leaders: A vision for change and hope.* Lanham, MD: Rowman & Littlefield.

Greene, M. (1998). Towards beginnings. In W. F. Pinar (Ed.), *The passionate mind of Maxine Greene: "I am . . . not yet"* (pp. 256–57). London: Falmer Press.

Luce, E. (2017). *The retreat of western liberalism.* New York, NY: Atlantic Monthly Press.

Szymborska, W. (1996). Nobel lecture: *The New Republic,* December 10.

Ulgins, M., & Ylimaki, R. (Eds.). (2017). *Bridging educational leadership, curriculum theory and Didaktik: Non-affirmative theory of education.* Cham, Switzerland: Springer-Kluwer.

Index

About the Authors

James Henderson is professor of curriculum studies at Kent State University, where he holds the Rebecca Tolle and Burton W. Gorman Chair in Educational Leadership. His publications address the topics of reflective teaching, transformative curriculum leadership, democratic collegial study, curriculum wisdom, curriculum-based pedagogy, and reconceptualized curriculum development.

Daniel Castner is assistant professor of early childhood education and teacher leadership at Bellarmine University in Louisville, Kentucky. His scholarship addresses teachers' endeavors to enact and lead democratic curriculum and pedagogy amidst the era of standardization and accountability.

Jennifer Schneider is doctoral candidate in curriculum and instruction at Kent State University with an academic and teaching background in art education, art history, and English education. Her scholarly interests dwell in aesthetics, everyday life, and holistic education.